Ultimate FACTIVITY Collection

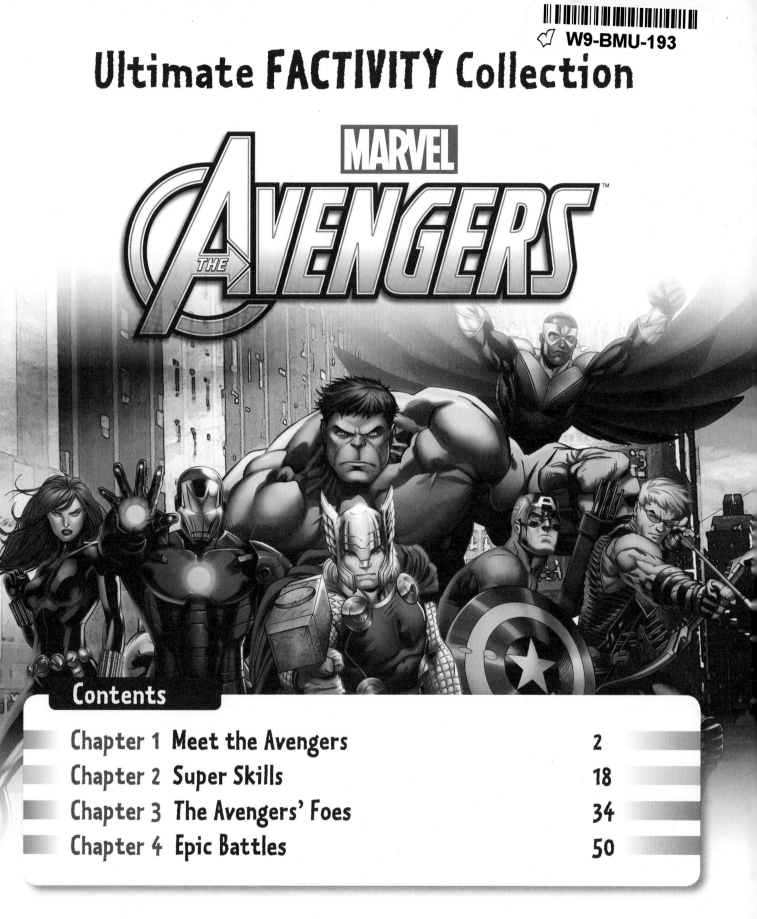

MARVEL

THE AVENGERS

Contents

This book belongs to:

✎ _____

CHAPTER 1 Meet the Avengers

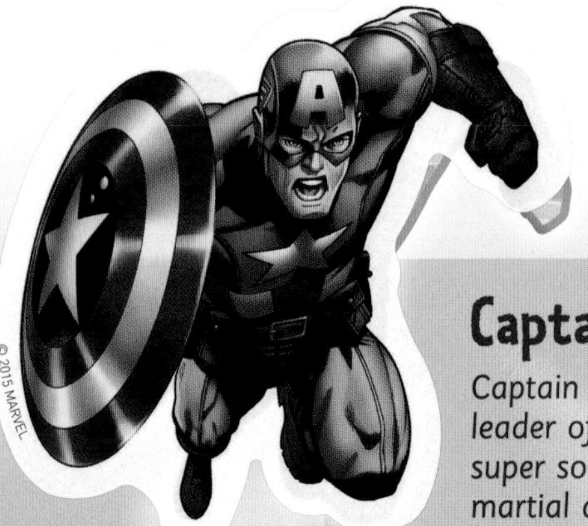
© 2015 MARVEL

Captain America

Captain America is often the leader of the Avengers. This super soldier is an expert in martial arts and is extremely strong.

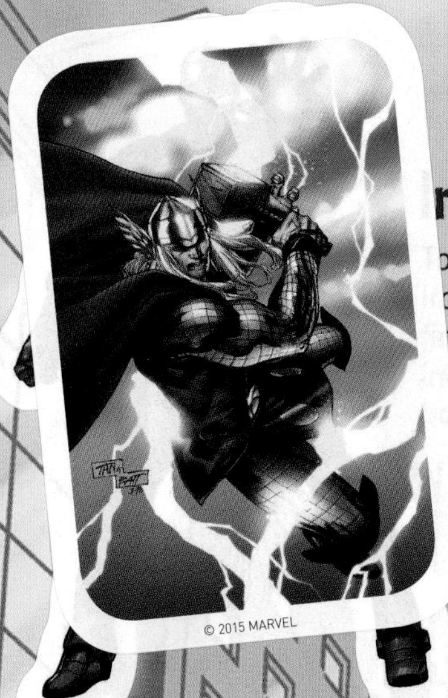
© 2015 MARVEL

ron Man

ony Stark, better known as on Man, was one of the st Avengers. He uses credible technology in ttle to beat his foes.

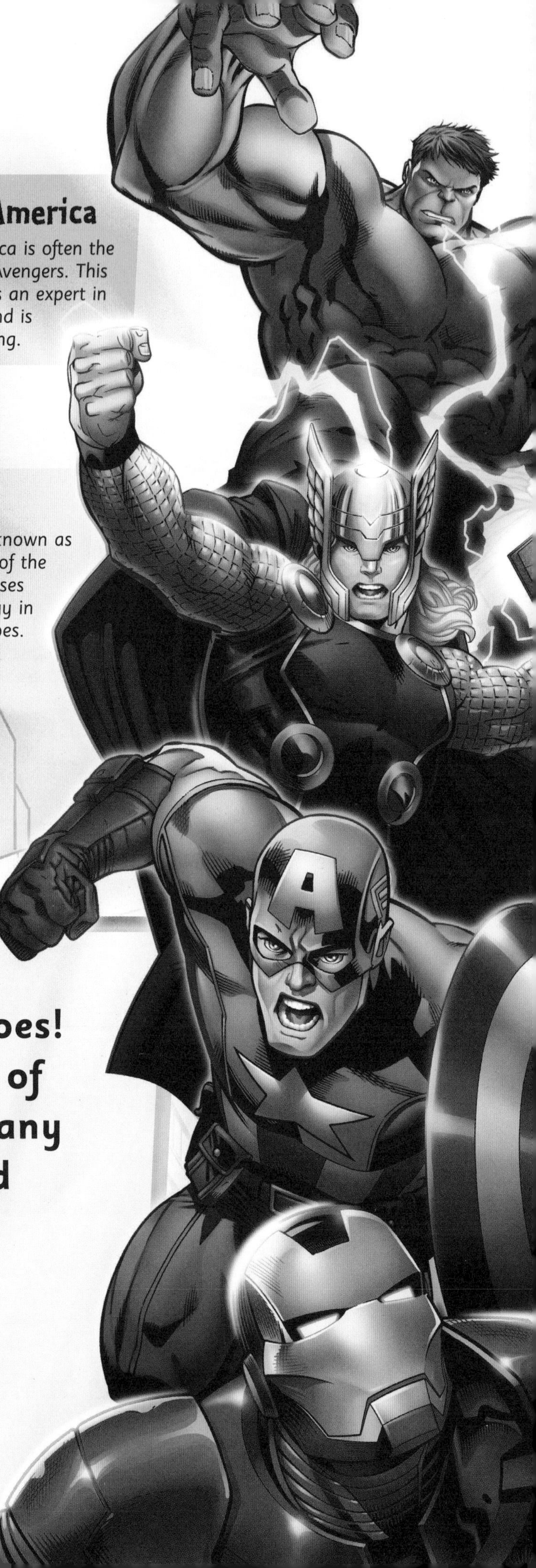

The Avengers are Earth's mightiest heroes! The team is made up of Super Heroes with many incredible powers and skills. They work together to keep Earth safe by taking down enemies that they could not defeat alone.

Find the **stickers** at the back of the book.

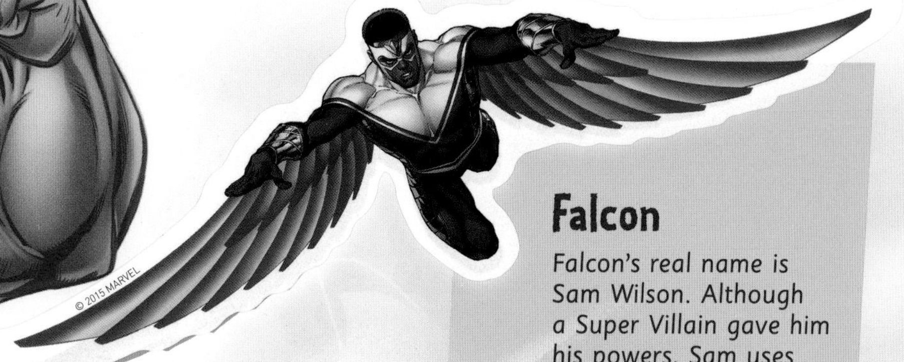
© 2015 MARVEL

Falcon

Falcon's real name is Sam Wilson. Although a Super Villain gave him his powers, Sam uses them to fight evil.

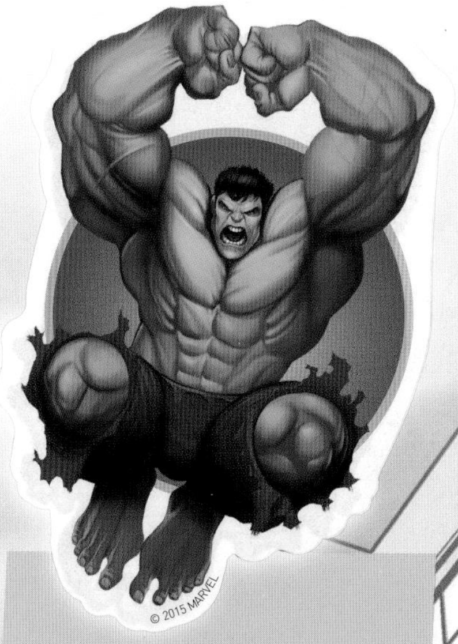
© 2015 MARVEL

The Hulk

When Bruce Banner loses control, he changes into the super-strong and incredibly angry Hulk.

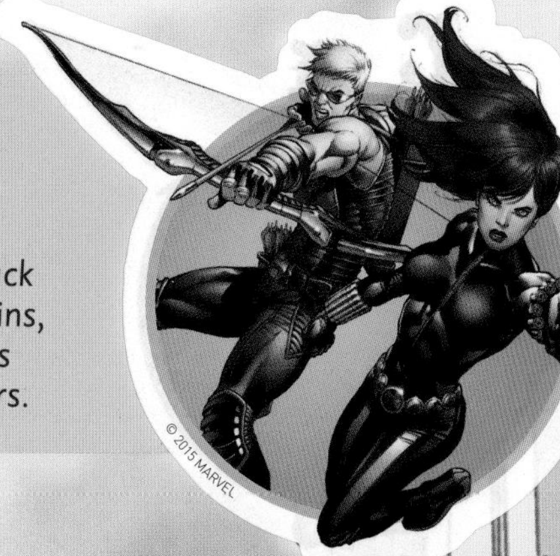
© 2015 MARVEL

Black Widow and Hawkeye

Both Hawkeye and Black Widow were once villains, but they swapped sides and joined the Avengers.

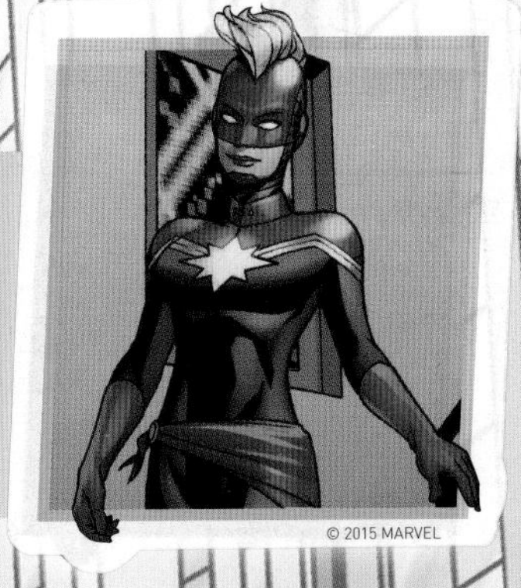
© 2015 MARVEL

Captain Marvel

Carol Danvers, also known as Captain Marvel, is part-alien and has many special powers.

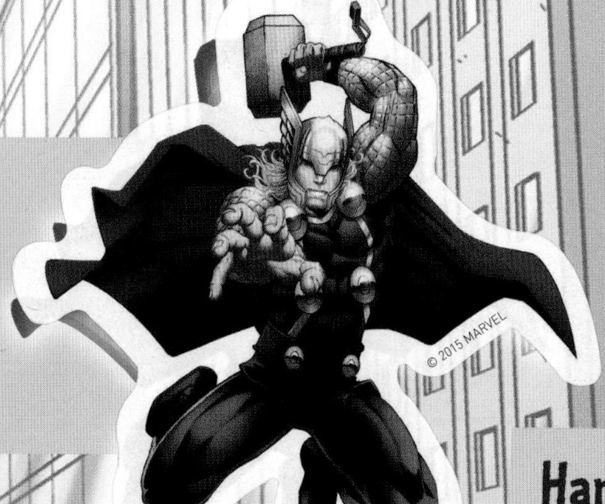
© 2015 MARVEL

Thor

Thor is a prince of the realm of Asgard. He is super-strong, can fly, and has a mystical hammer called Mjolnir.

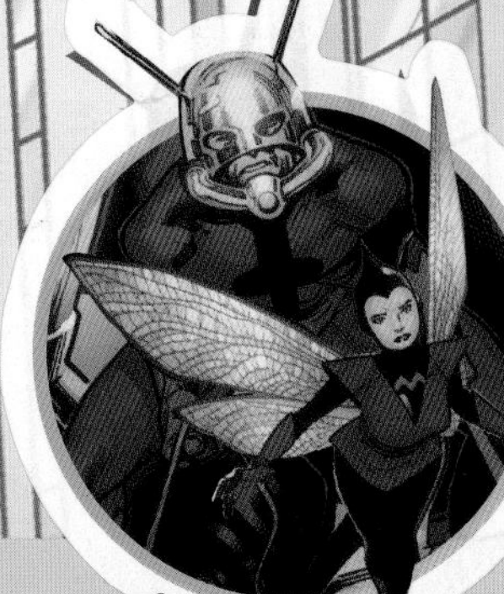
© 2015 MARVEL

Hank Pym and Wasp

Both these Super Heroes have the amazing ability to alter their size.

Captain America

Fill in the speech bubbles

Captain America often leads the Avengers into battle. One of the team's earliest battles was against the Lava Men—terrifying monsters with fiery tempers that live deep underground.

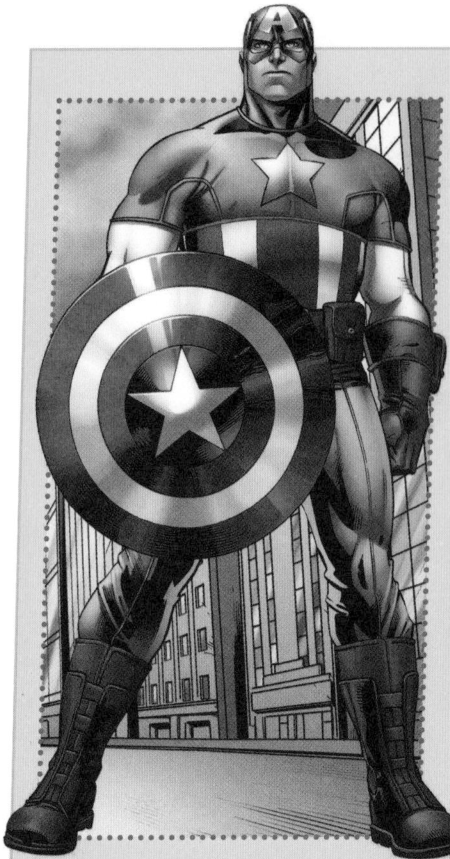

Great soldier

Captain America's real name is Steve Rogers. After he took the Super-Soldier Serum, his strength increased to the highest possible level for a human.

You could **write** in pencil first and then use a pen.

Decide what each character will say and write it in the blank speech bubbles.

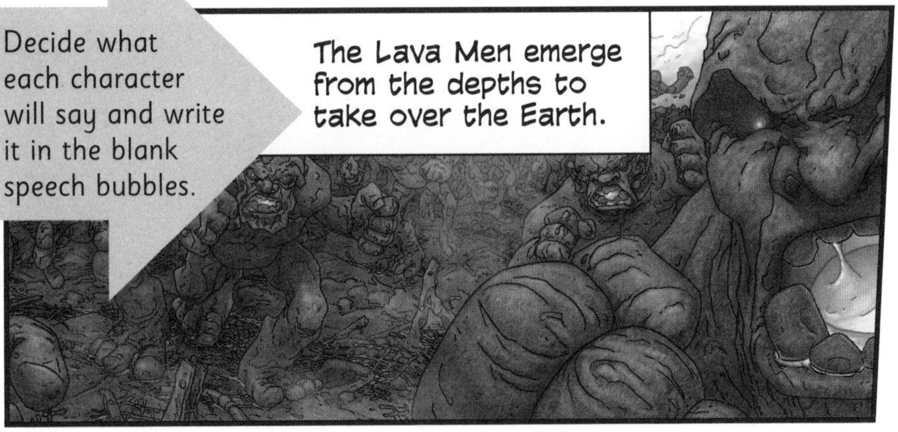

The Lava Men emerge from the depths to take over the Earth.

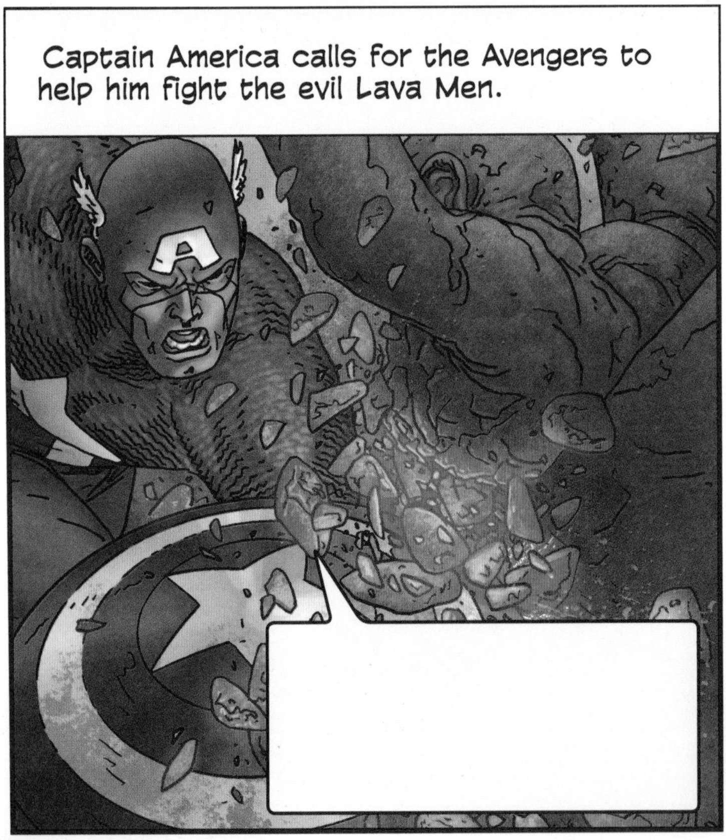

Captain America calls for the Avengers to help him fight the evil Lava Men.

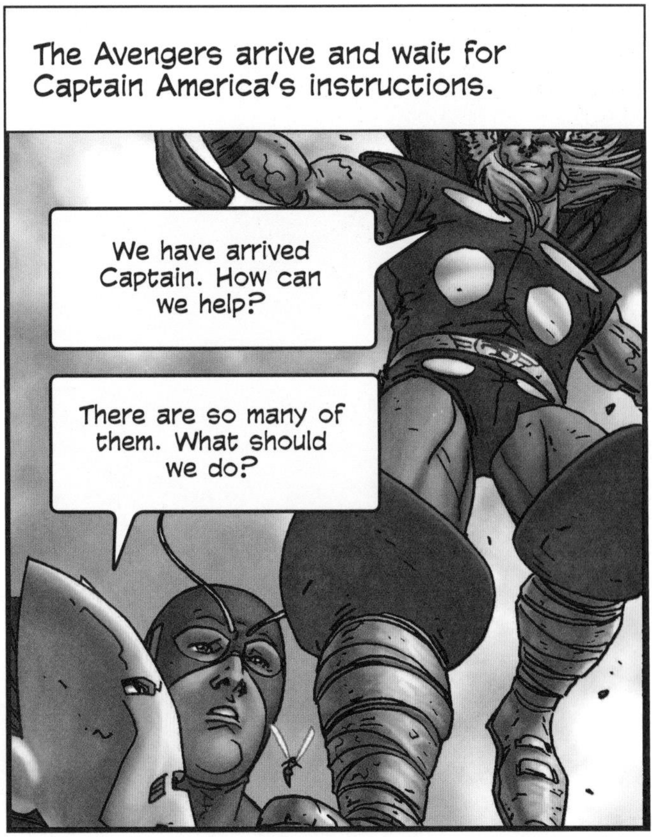

The Avengers arrive and wait for Captain America's instructions.
We have arrived Captain. How can we help?
There are so many of them. What should we do?

Read and Create

Use the **jagged shapes** to add comic book noises, like "crash!"

As he struggles to hold back the Lava Men, Captain America asks Iron Man for help.

Iron Man uses all his might to create a wall. This annoys the Lava Men!

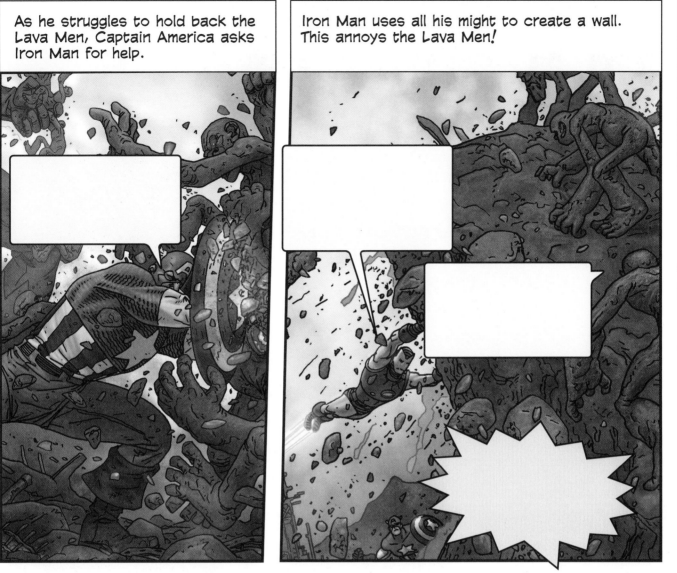

The angry Lava Men get past the wall that Iron Man has built! Captain America calls upon Giant Man for help. Can he help drive the Lava Men back underground?!

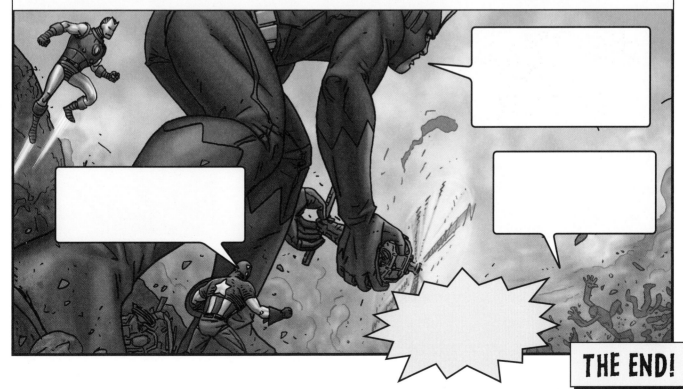

THE END!

Iron Man

Design new armor for Iron Man

Tony Stark, also known as Iron Man, is a technological genius. He has designed and built many different armored suits that give him superhuman abilities. Each suit has its own strengths, weapons, and powers.

Read about some of Iron Man's armors, then design a new suit.

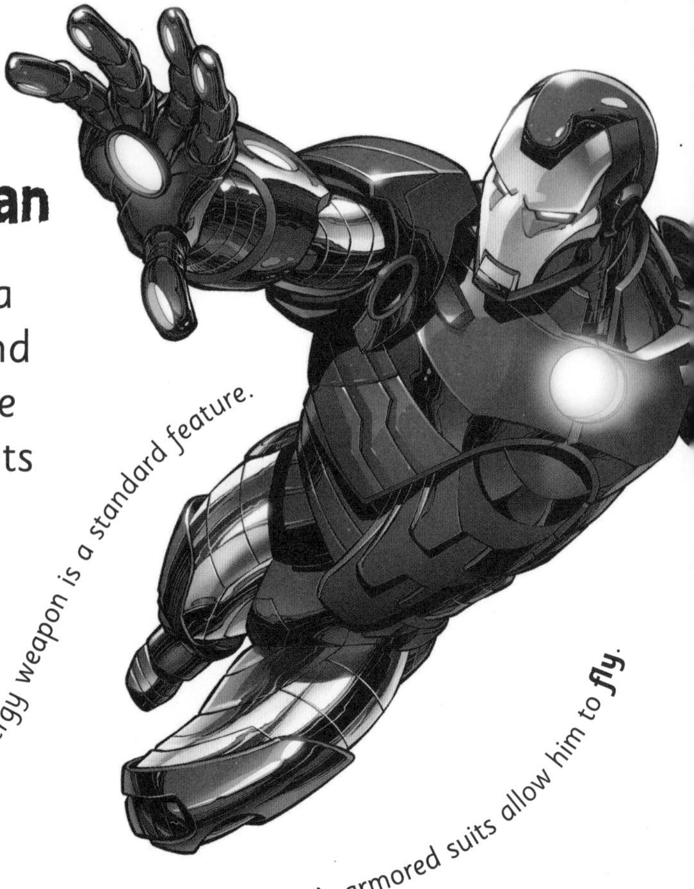

The palm-mounted **uni-beam** energy weapon is a standard feature.

Most of Iron Man's armored suits allow him to ***fly***.

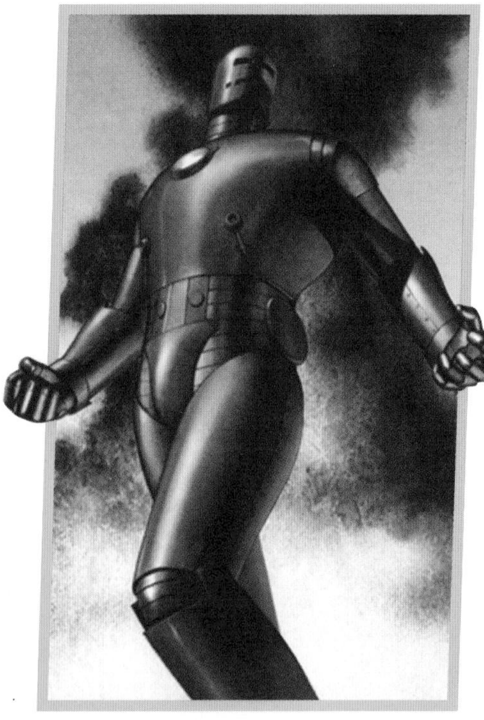

MK I Armor

This was Iron Man's first armor, which he built out of junk while being held prisoner. It is bulletproof and can use its built-in magnets to fire iron objects at enemies.

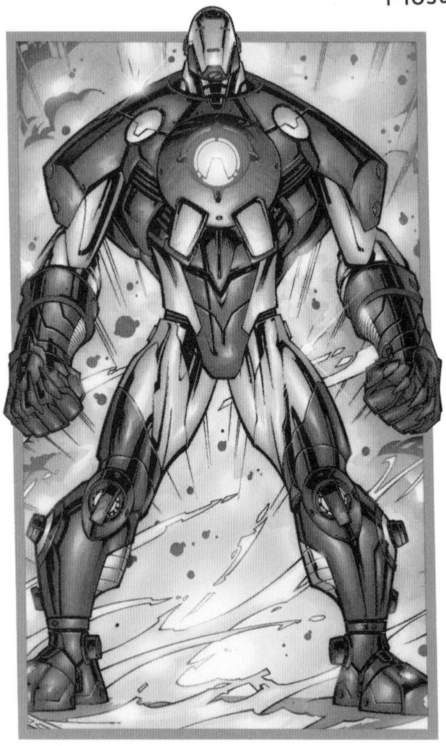

S.K.I.N. Armor

This armor is made of S.K.I.N., a special alloy that is super-flexible but also incredibly hard. The suit has powerful energy-blade weapons, and uses its own super-smart computer brain.

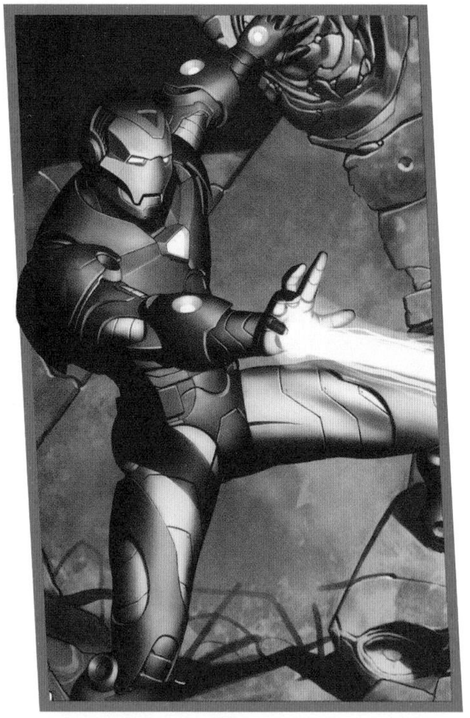

Extremis Armor

Stark designed this armor in order to use a techno-organic virus called Extremis. This armor can make itself invisible, has built-in shields, and can fire small explosives from its hands.

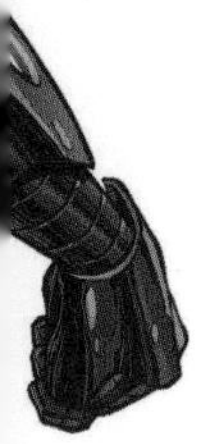

What **colors** will your armor be?

Will your suit include any special **weapons?**

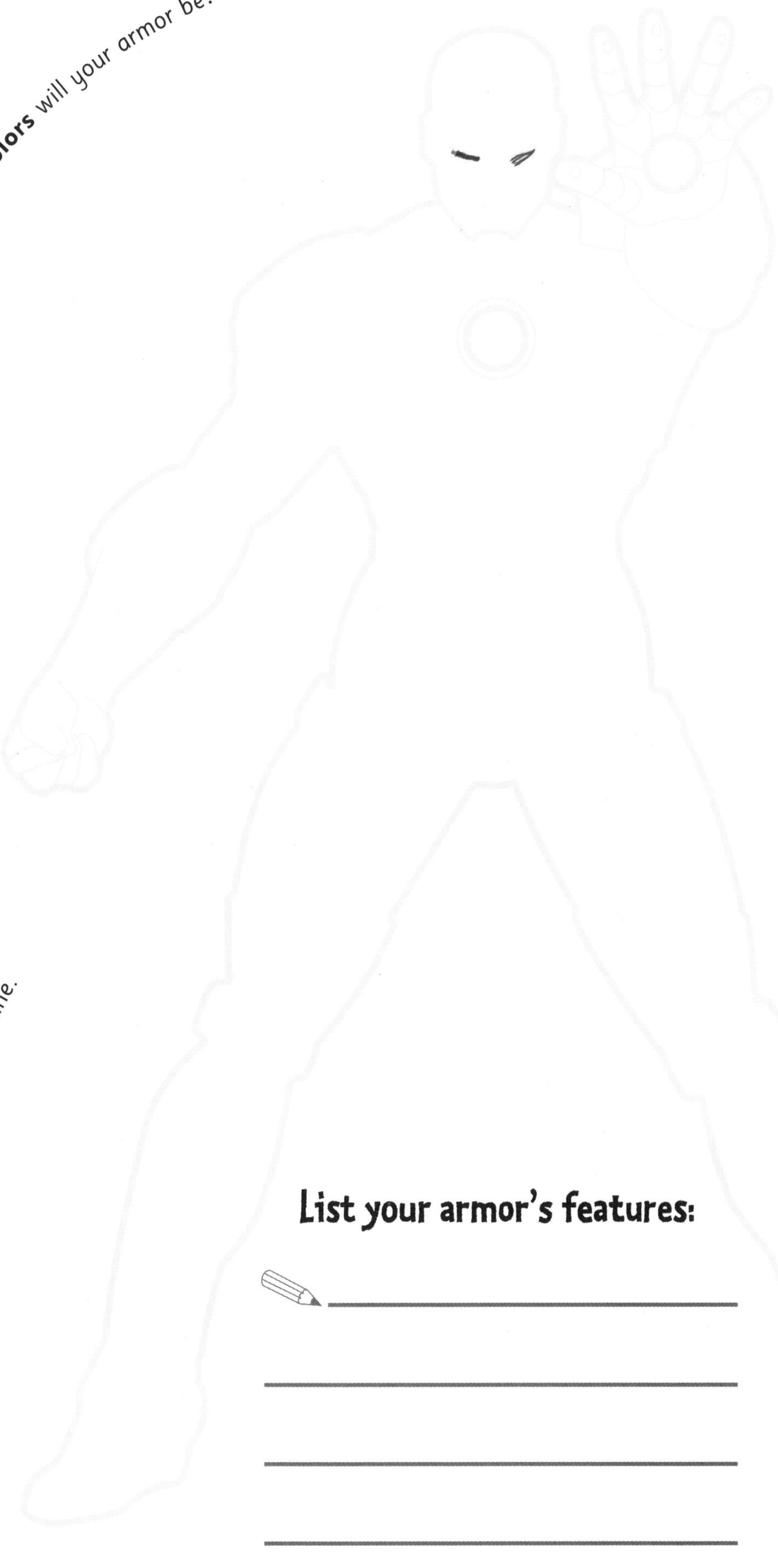

Draw your new armor's **details** inside the outline.

Where is **Iron Man** standing? You could fill in the **background**, too!

List your armor's features:

Go Team!

Spot the Avengers

The Avengers fight together as a team, but they all have different powers and abilities. Some are super-strong and acrobatic, others are amazingly fast, incredibly tough, or can fly!

Read about these Avengers, then use the clues to identify them.

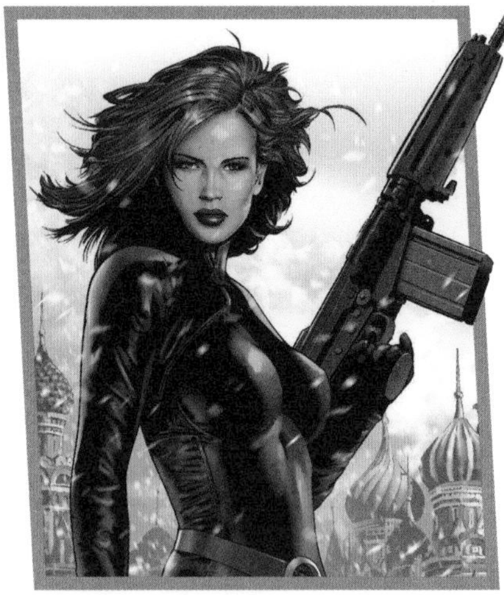

Black Widow

Black Widow was originally a spy who fought against the Avengers but later joined them. She is super-strong and a martial-arts expert.

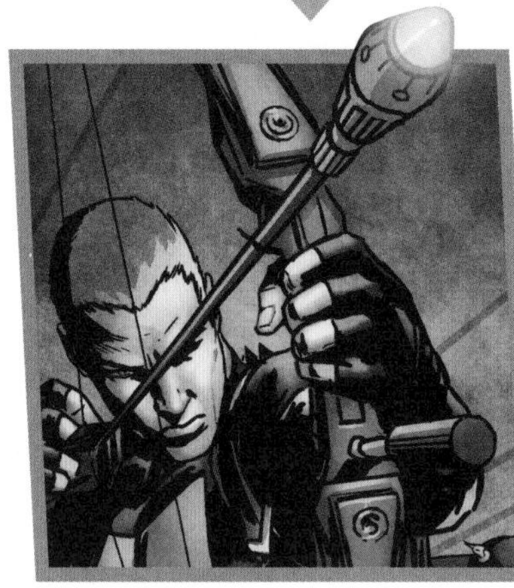

Hawkeye

Hawkeye trained as a circus performer. He is one of the best marksmen in the world, and is also a highly skilled acrobat.

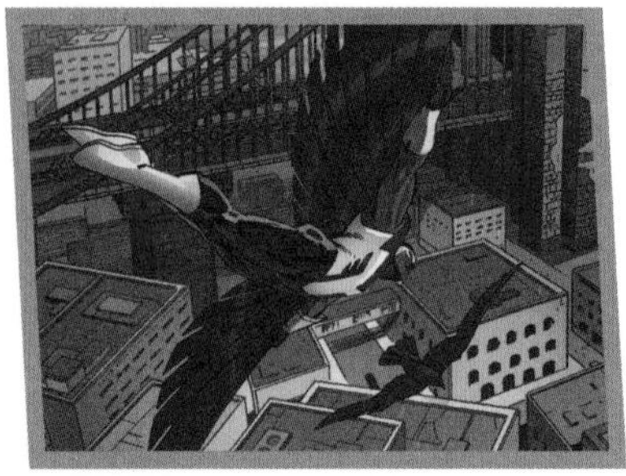

Falcon

Falcon grew up in Harlem in New York City. He can mentally link with birds, and wears a special harness that allows him to fly.

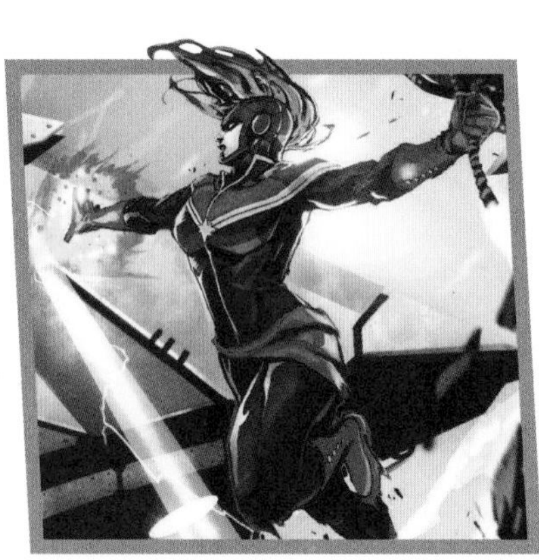

Captain Marvel

Captain Marvel got her powers from an alien race called the Kree. She has superhuman strength, can fly, and can fire energy from her fingers!

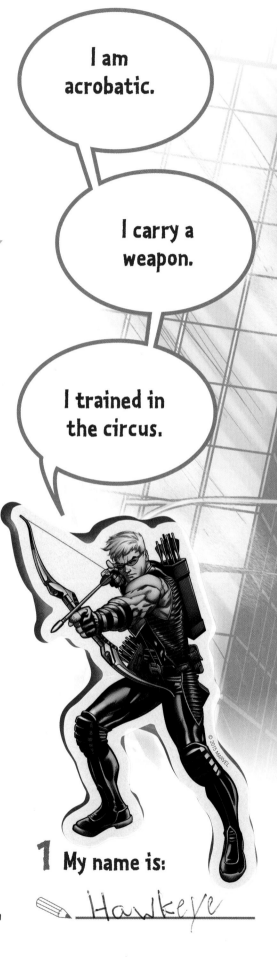

I am acrobatic.

I carry a weapon.

I trained in the circus.

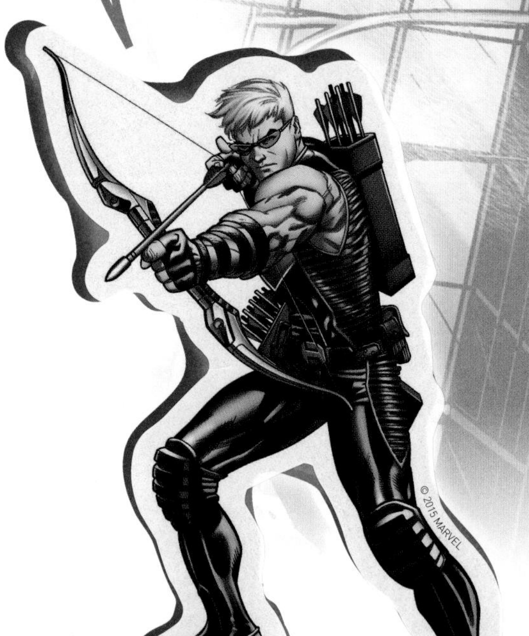
© 2015 MARVEL

1 My name is:

Hawkeye

Find the **stickers** at the back of the book.

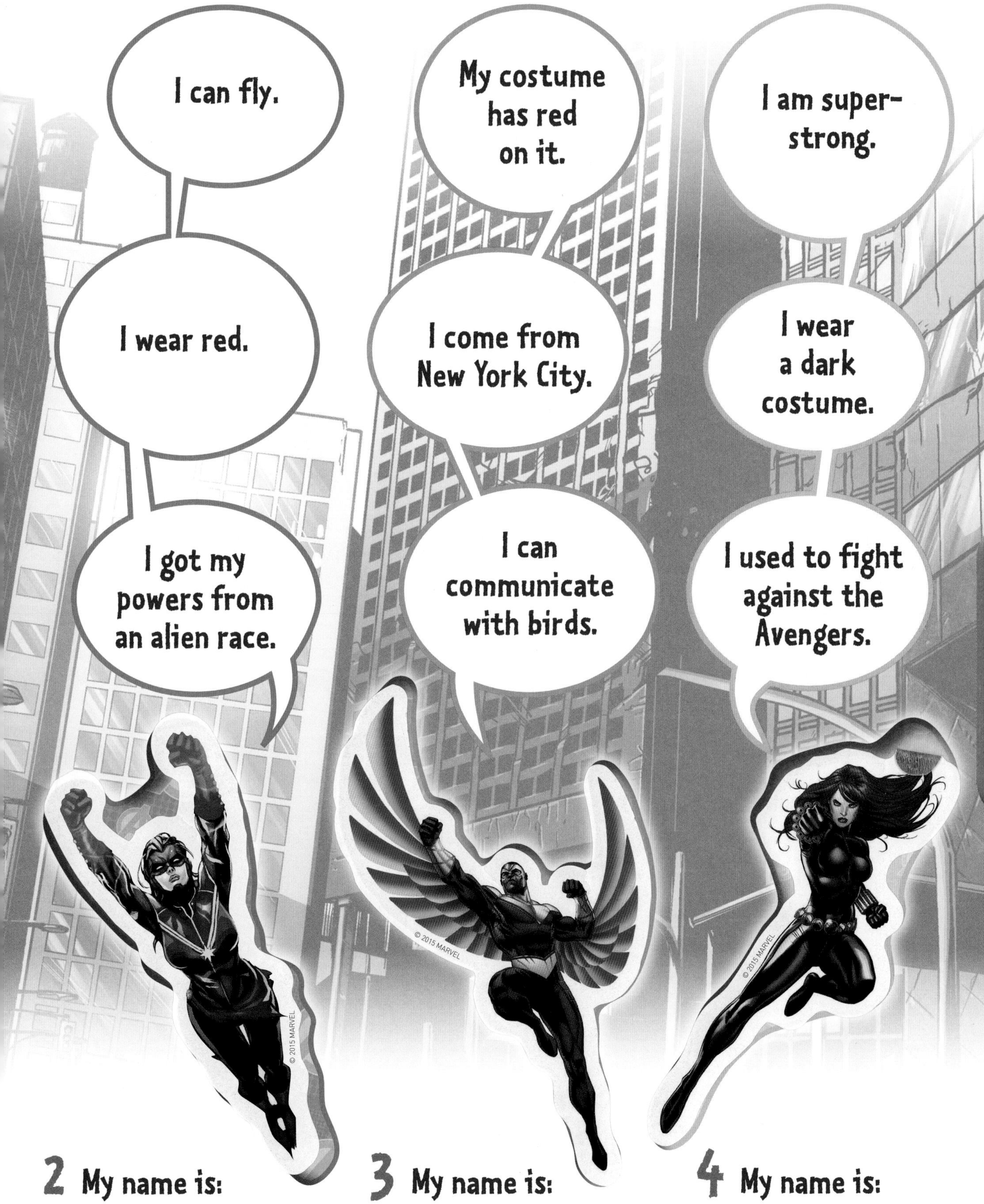
I can fly.
I wear red.
I got my powers from an alien race.
My costume has red on it.
I come from New York City.
I can communicate with birds.
I am super-strong.
I wear a dark costume.
I used to fight against the Avengers.
© 2015 MARVEL
© 2015 MARVEL
© 2015 MARVEL

2 My name is: Captain Marvel

3 My name is: Falcon

4 My name is: Black widow

Find the **answers** on page 97.

A New Avenger
Design a new Super Hero

Over the years, many different Super Heroes have joined the Avengers. All of them have incredible skills or super-powers that have helped the team. The Avengers always look for new recruits to help protect Earth.

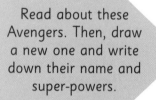

Read about these Avengers. Then, draw a new one and write down their name and super-powers.

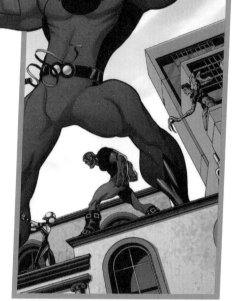

Hank Pym

Hank Pym can tower above buildings or become as small as an ant. He also designed an amazing helmet that lets him communicate with insects.

Vision

This noble robot can change his body, so he can become as tough as a diamond or so light that he can fly. Vision can also fire energy blasts.

Wasp

Janet Van Dyne can shrink down to a tiny size. She can also grow insect-like wings out of her back and fire energy bolts from her hands.

Black Panther

Black Panther has superhuman senses. His costume is bulletproof, and his strong, Vibranium claws can cut through any metal.

Draw the Super Hero's **portrait in here.**

THE AVENGERS

Identicard

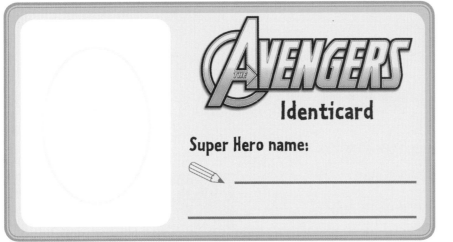

Super Hero name:

____

____

*Write down what **powers** your Super Hero has. How about the ability to control water or the power to see into the future?*

____

____

____

You could show your Super Hero **in battle or using their powers.**

You could add **gadgets** to the costume, like a flame thrower.

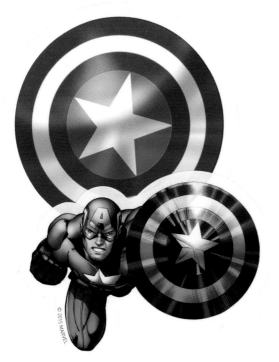

© 2015 MARVEL

A **mask** and **costume** will hide your new Super Hero's identity.

Angry Hulk

Stick Hulk back together!

Learn about the Hulk, then complete the picture of him using sticker pieces.

Bruce Banner has the amazing ability to change into the Hulk. The Hulk is one of the strongest Avengers, but also the most unpredictable. Bruce and the Hulk have been Avengers ever since the team first assembled.

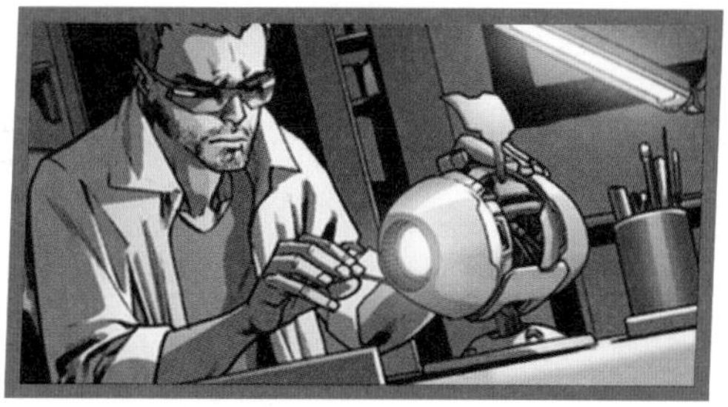

Dr. Banner

Bruce is a brilliant scientist. When he is not beating up villains as the Hulk, Banner loves using his mind to solve difficult problems for the Avengers.

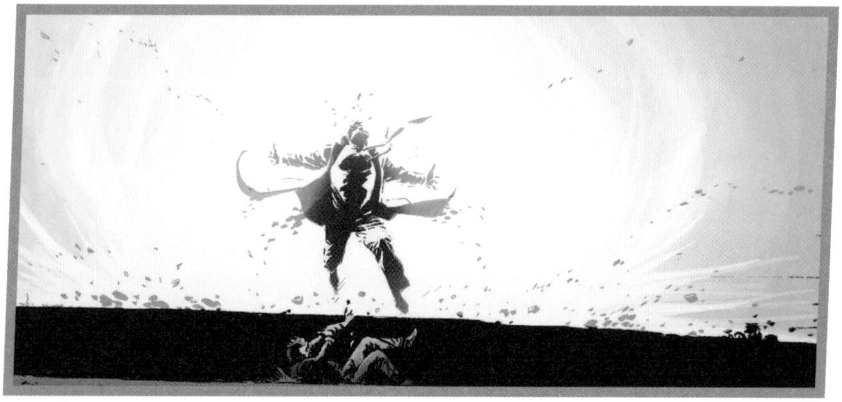

The birth of the Hulk

Bruce was testing a powerful gamma bomb when teenager Rick Jones wandered onto the test site. Bruce managed to protect Rick from the explosion, but could not save himself. He received a blast of gamma radiation that changed him forever.

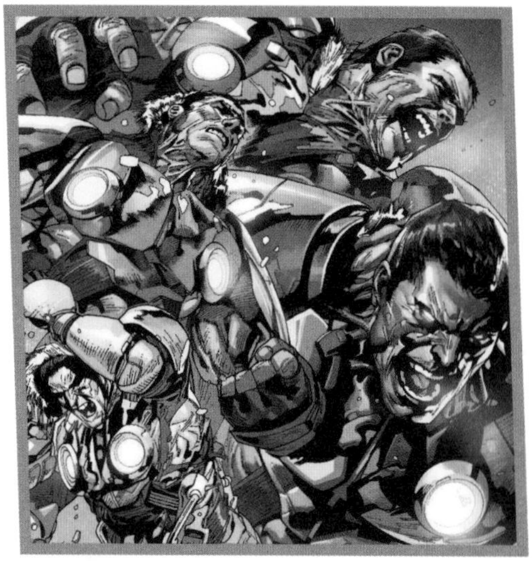

Going green

Whenever Bruce's anger reaches a certain level, he transforms from a normal man into a towering, muscly, green monster and gains many amazing super-powers.

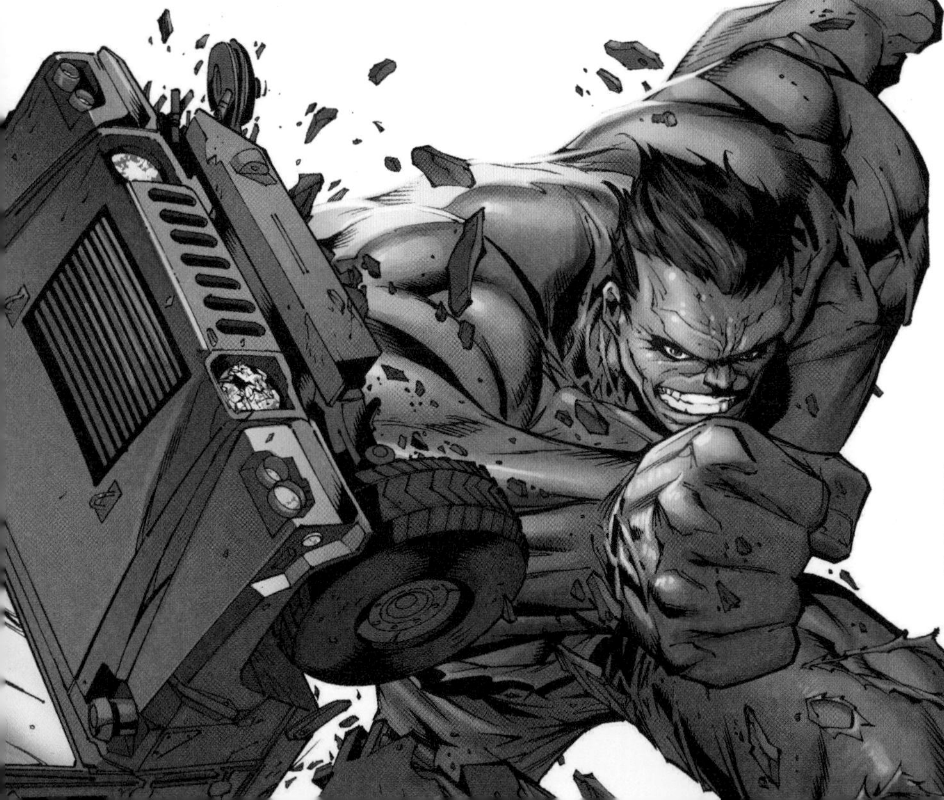

Hulk smash!

Hulk's strength is off the charts, and it increases as he gets angrier. The Hulk can heal really quickly. Also, his green skin is super-tough. The Hulk's awesome powers mean that villains best watch out!

Find the **stickers** at the back of the book.

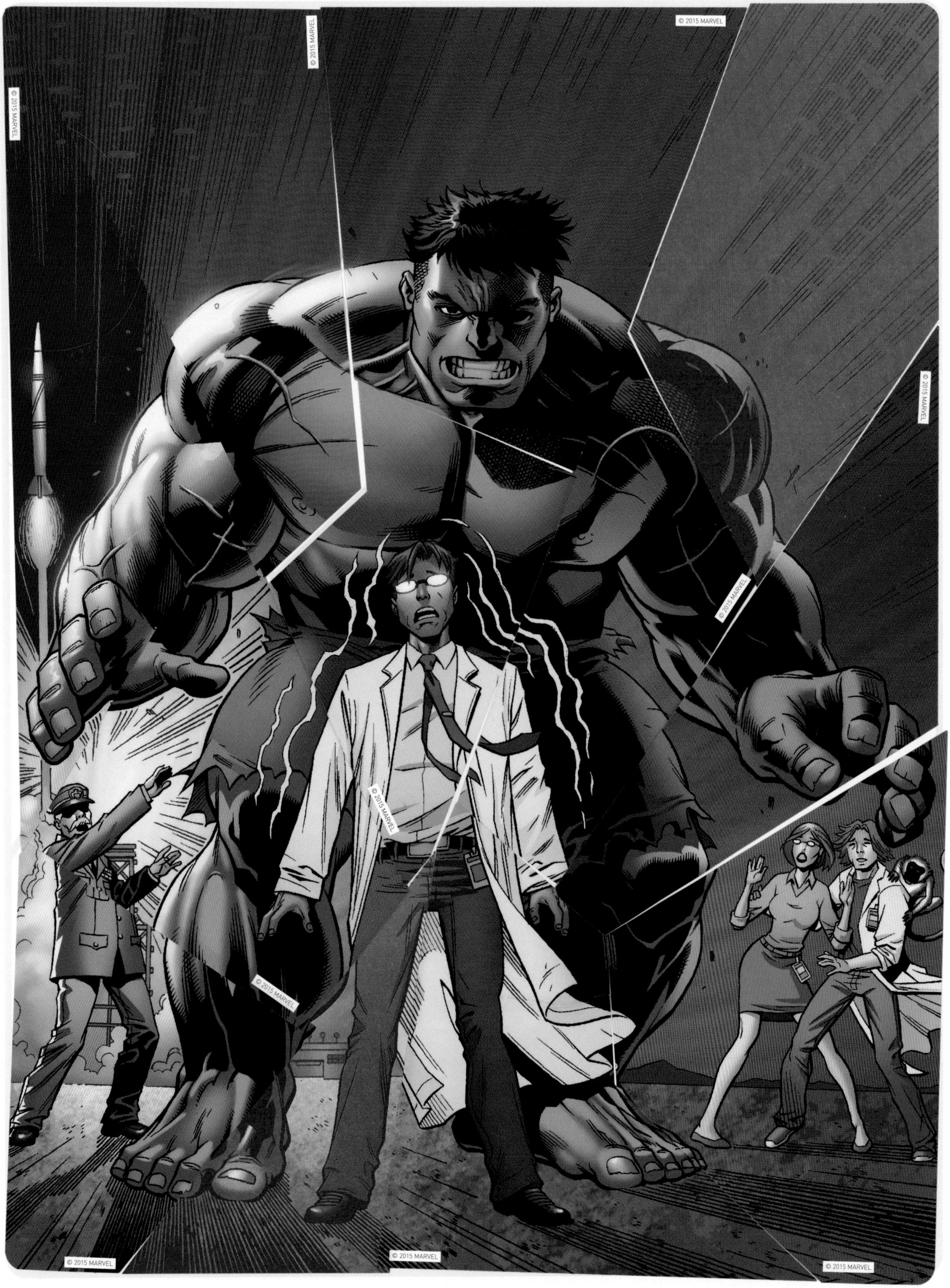

© 2015 MARVEL
© 2015 MARVEL
© 2015 MARVEL
© 2015 MARVEL
© 2015 MARVEL
© 2015 MARVEL
© 2015 MARVEL
© 2015 MARVEL
© 2015 MARVEL
© 2015 MARVEL

Bruce turns a bright shade of **green** when he is in a rage!

Fact Challenge

The Hulk has enormous **muscles**.

The Avengers' Charter

Read about the Avengers' Charter and fill in the blanks on the scroll.

Fill in the blanks

The Avengers are bound by a charter that they must follow at all times. Before any new Avenger can join the team, they must read the charter and agree to live by its rules.

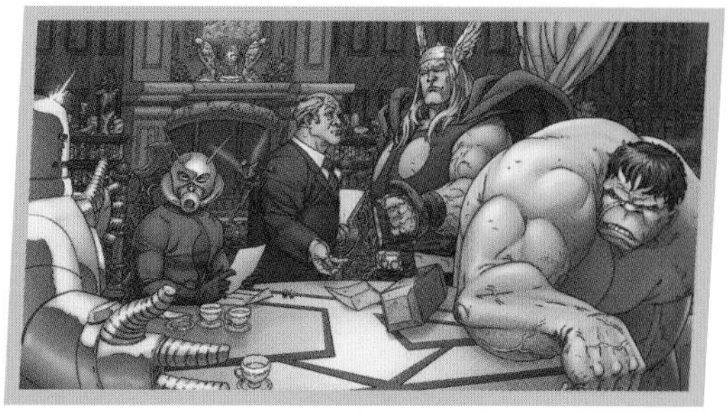

Founding Avengers

After their first mission, the original Avengers agreed that they would protect Earth from any threat. They also decided that Avengers must always use their powers for good causes.

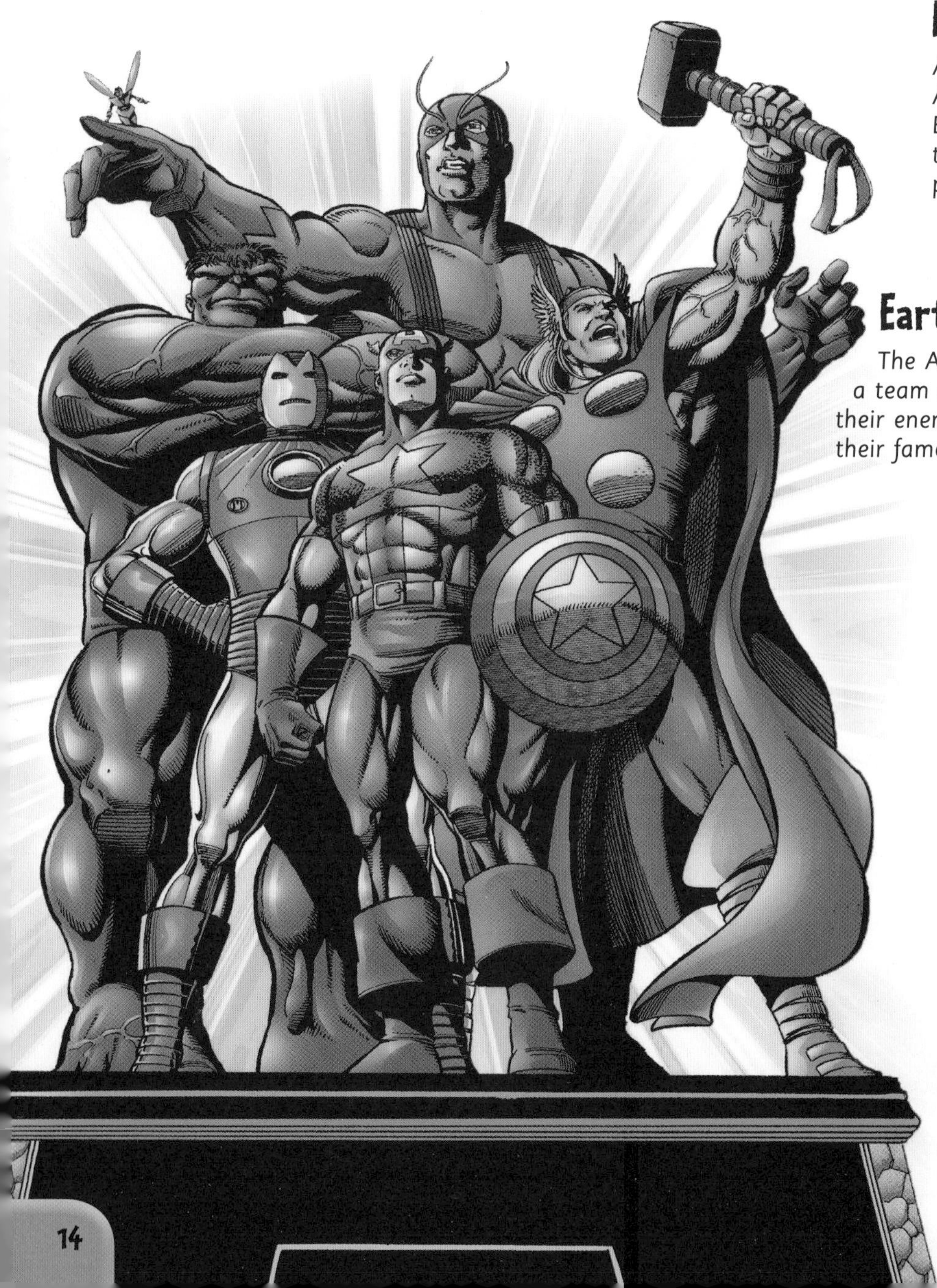

Earth's Mightiest Heroes

The Avengers have to work well in a team and respect each other to defeat their enemies. All Avengers must answer their famous call: "Avengers assemble!"

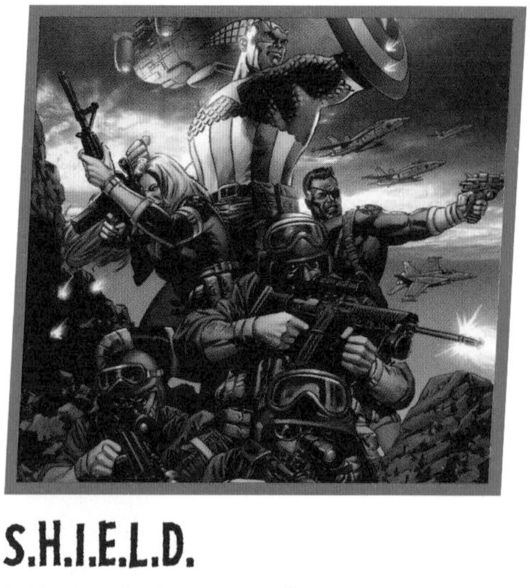

S.H.I.E.L.D.

S.H.I.E.L.D. is a United Nations agency responsible for protecting humanity. Some Super Villains are too tough for S.H.I.E.L.D. to handle alone, so they ask the Avengers for help.

The Avengers'
Official Charter

1 The Avengers must protect our planet from any _____ .

2 All Super Heroes must use their powers for _____ causes.

3 Avengers must respect each other and work well in a _____ .

4 Avengers must help the United Nations agency _____ to protect humanity.

5 Avengers must always answer the call: _____ !

Fact Challenge

Find the **answers** on page 97.

Find the **sticker** of the Avengers' symbol at the back of the book to seal the scroll.

Chapter 1 Challenge

Test your knowledge of this chapter

Answer each question. If you need help, look back through the section.

Now you have finished the first chapter of the book, take the Challenge to find out if you are an expert!

1. Find the sticker that best matches the description:

This Super Hero created a suit of Extremis Armor.

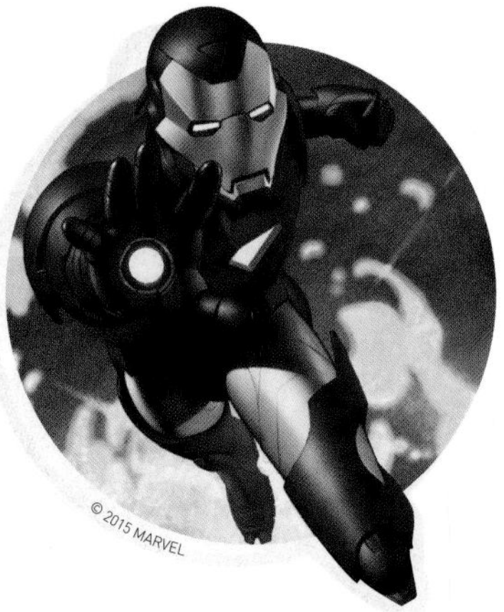
© 2015 MARVEL

2. What kind of weapon is Thor's Mjolnir?

Club ☐ **Hammer** ☑ **Sword** ☐

3. The Avengers do not have to obey the rules of their charter all of the time.

True ☑ **False** ☐

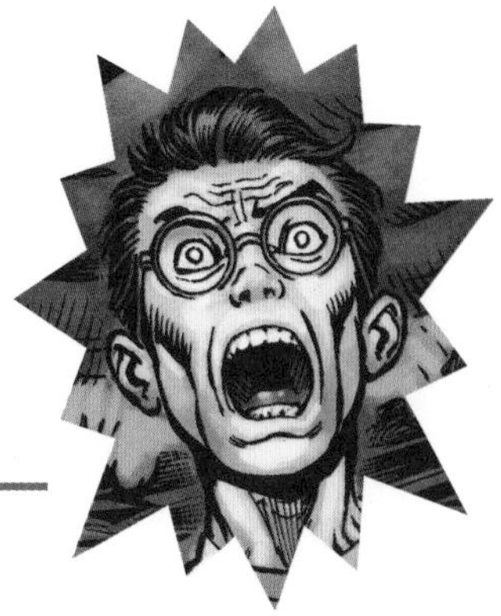

4. What is this name of this person, who can turn into the Hulk? ✏ Bruce Banner

5. Black Panther's Vibranium claws are able to slice through any ✏ metal.

Find the **answers** on page 97.

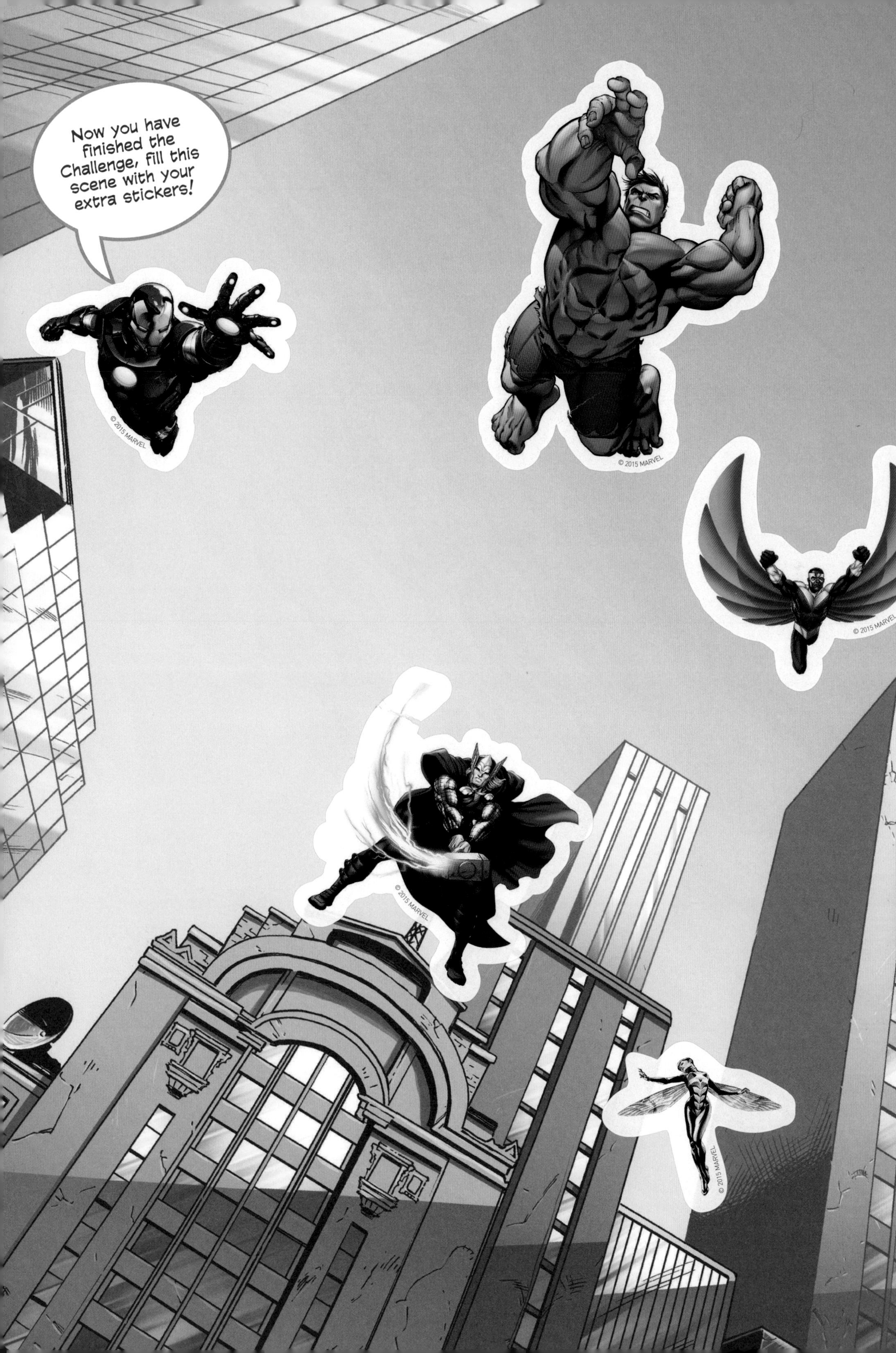
Now you have finished the Challenge, fill this scene with your extra stickers!
© 2015 MARVEL

CHAPTER 2 Super Skills

The Avengers fight together as a team, but they each have different skills and weapons. This makes them even stronger—if a villain manages to resist one hero's powers, the other Avengers can jump in with theirs and help to defeat them!

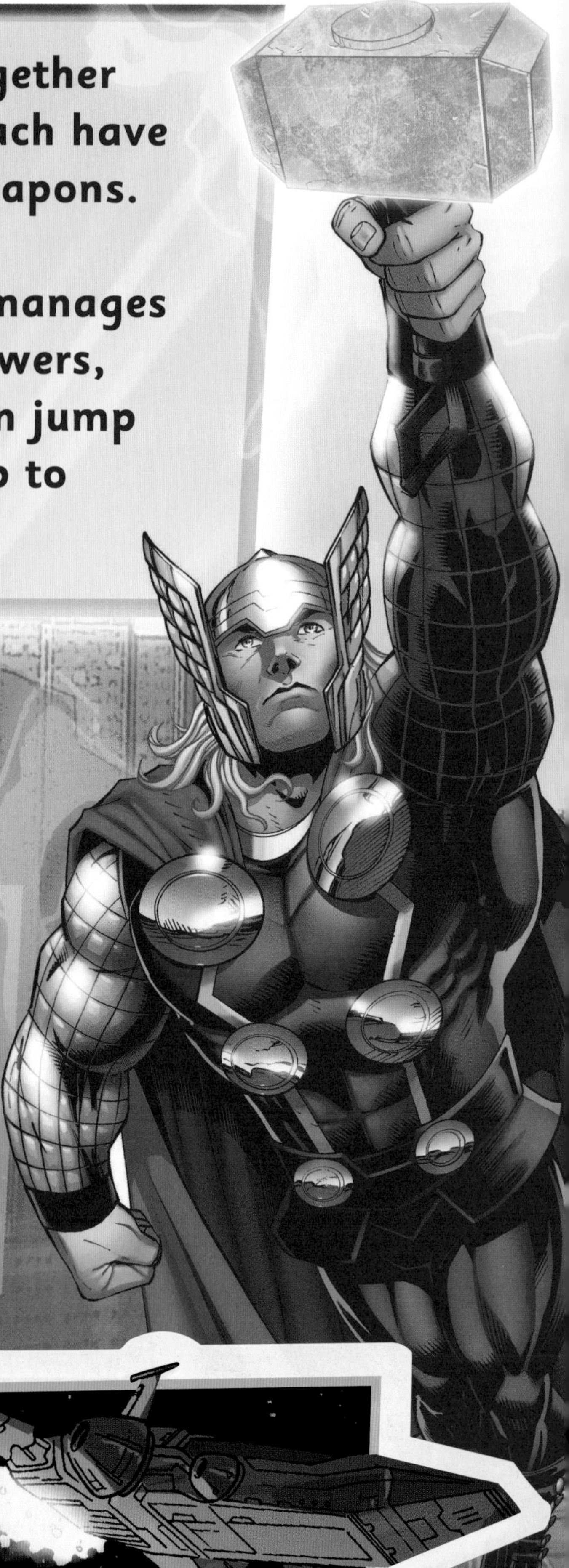

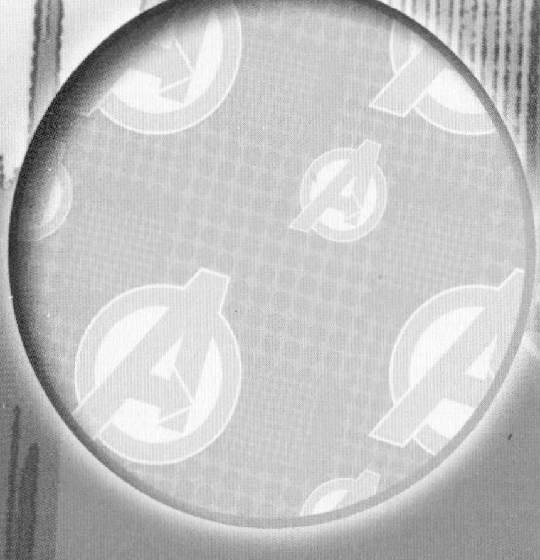

Cap's shield

Captain America always carries his shield into battle. This amazing tool is made of a very strong metal called Vibranium. It can even withstand a hit from Thor's hammer!

The Quinjet

When there is trouble, the Avengers need to travel fast! The Quinjet is their personal shuttle. It carries them quickly into battle, no matter where the conflict is.

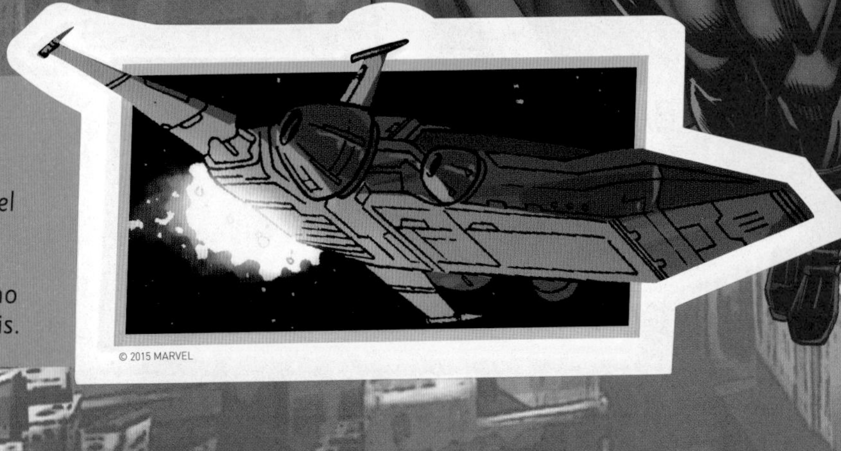

Find the **stickers** at the back of the book.

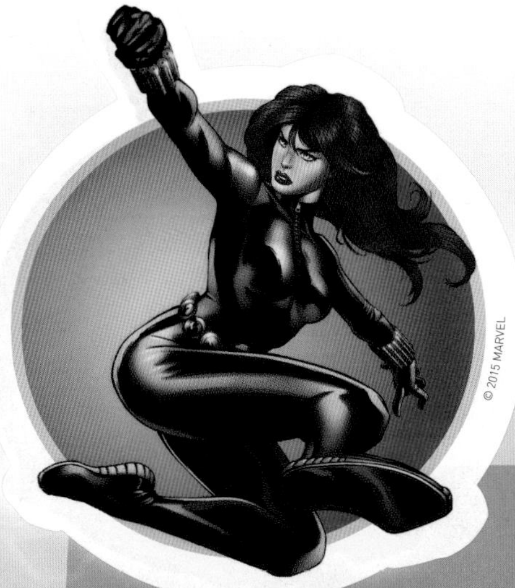
© 2015 MARVEL

Captain Marvel

Captain Marvel is one of the most powerful Avengers. Her part-human, part-alien DNA gives her awesome powers. She can fly and fire energy blasts that are as strong as a nuclear bomb!

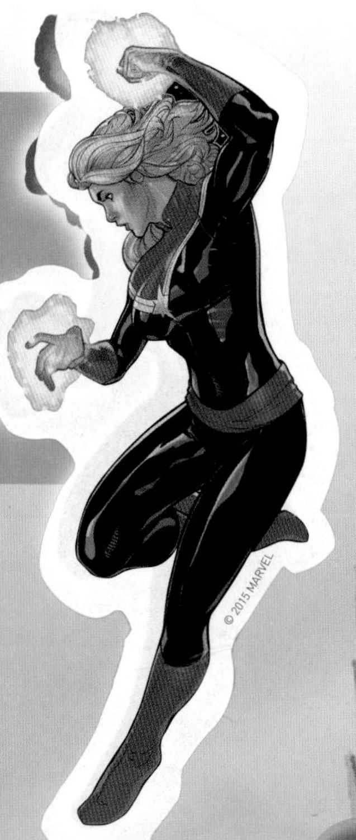
© 2015 MARVEL

Black Widow

This secretive super-spy isn't afraid of anything! The Super-Soldier Serum has given her amazing strength and acrobatic skills. Her special spy gear is powerful and ultra-modern, too!

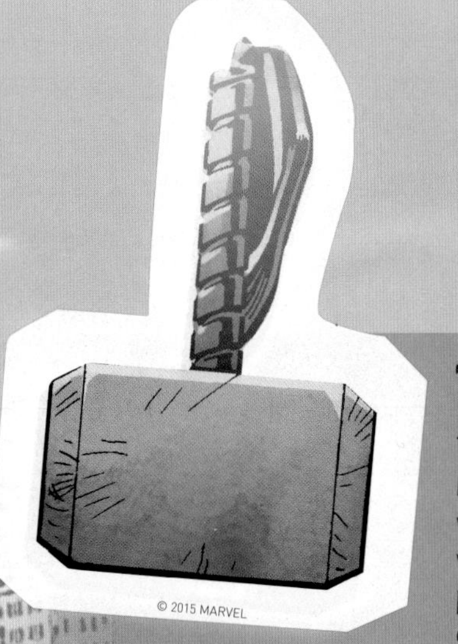
© 2015 MARVEL

Thor's hammer

Thor's hammer is called Mjolnir, which means "that which smashes." This mighty weapon has many special powers, and makes Thor almost invincible!

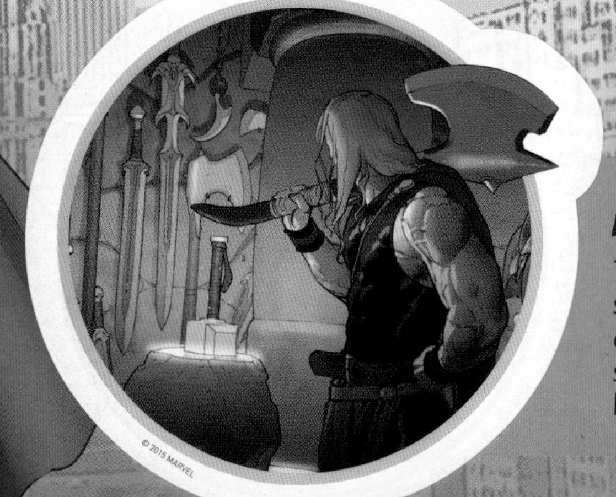
© 2015 MARVEL

Asgardian technology

The warriors of Asgard carry strange and powerful weapons and artifacts. Even the smartest scientists on Earth cannot understand how these mysterious tools work.

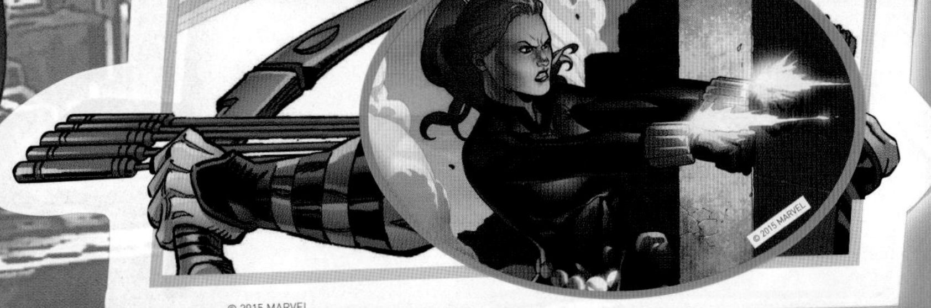
© 2015 MARVEL
© 2015 MARVEL

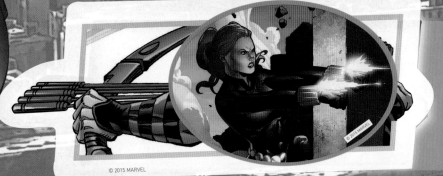

Hawkeye

Hawkeye has an unusual skill—he never misses! This makes him an amazing archer. Hawkeye doesn't always use normal arrows. At times he uses special trick arrows that he invents.

Asgard Weapons

Design a new weapon

The legends of the realm of Asgard are filled with stories of mighty weapons and the warriors who use them. These fearsome weapons have their own names, and each of them has awesome powers.

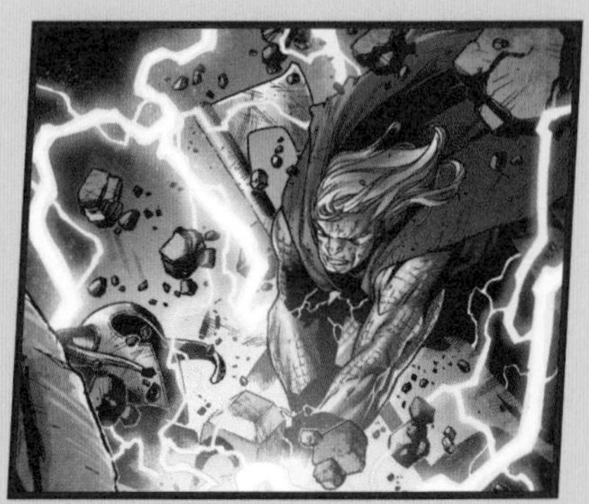

Thor Odinson

Thor is the god of thunder, and son of Odin, King of Asgard. He has fought as one of the Avengers many times, often to defend Earth from the evil schemes of his brother, Loki.

Read about these legendary weapons of Asgard, then design a new one.

The power of Thor

Thor is the only one who can use Mjolnir. Anyone else who tries would not even be able to pick it up!

Lord of strength

Thor is the strongest of the Asgardians. He once pushed over the Leaning Tower of Pisa with a single finger!

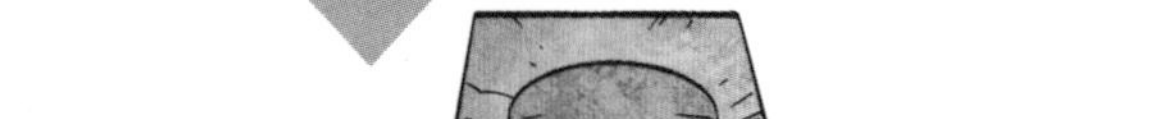

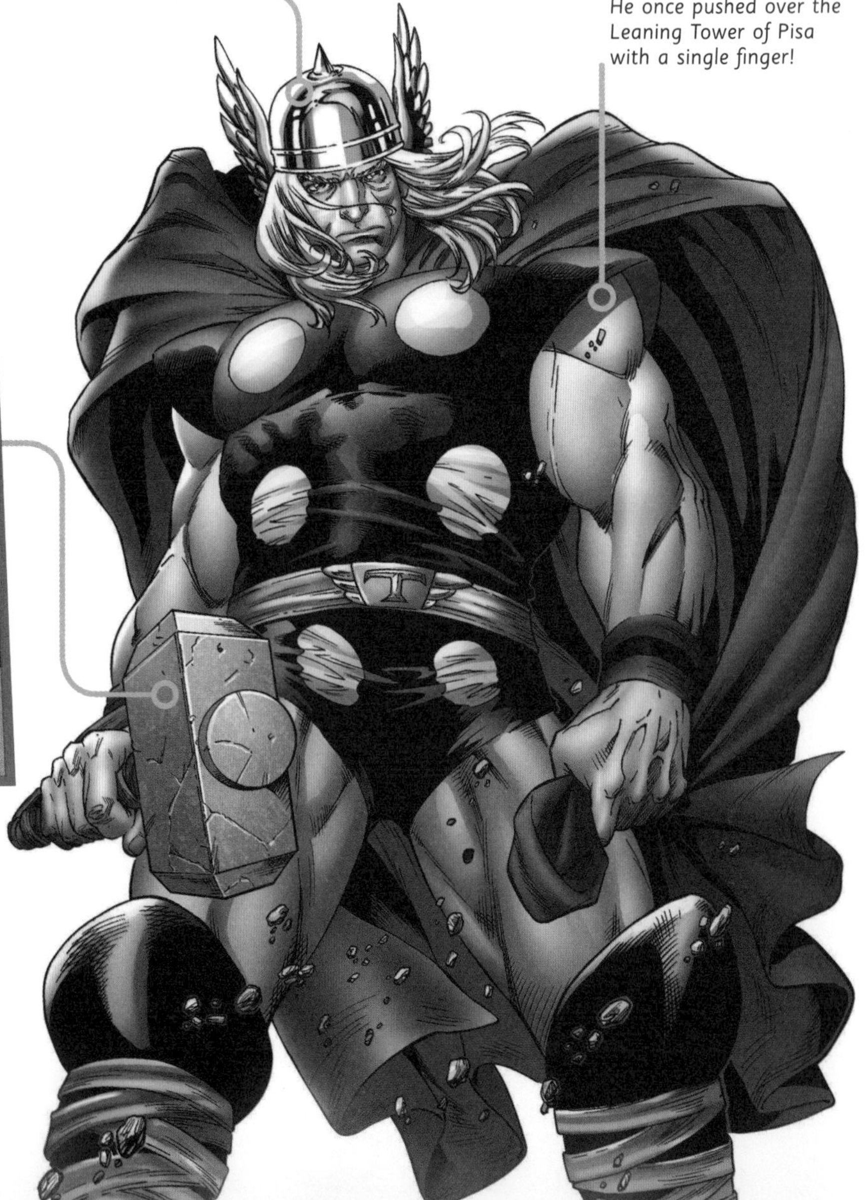

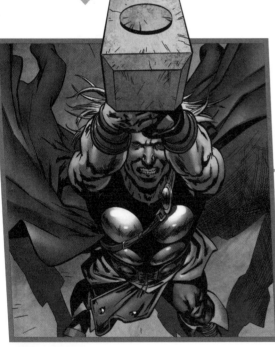

Mjolnir

The powerful hammer Mjolnir is indestructible. It gives Thor the power to summon lightning and the strength to crush mountains! Odin ordered this hammer to be forged from the core of a star. He gave it to Thor after he proved himself worthy of using it.

Jarnbjorn

Thor carried this ax before he was given Mjolnir. He eventually lost it, but it was found by the villain Kang the Conqueror. Its name means "Iron Bear."

Gungnir

Gungnir is the spear of Odin. It is made from an enchanted metal called Uru, and is a symbol of Odin's power. If Odin throws it, it will return to him.

Gram

This sword belonged to the legendary Asgardian warrior Sigurd, who used it to slay the dragon Fafnir. It was later claimed by Thor's brother, Loki.

What **type** of weapon will you draw?

What **decoration** does your weapon have on it?

What **special powers** does your weapon have?

This weapon is called:

Captain Marvel

Fill in the gaps

Read about Captain Marvel's powers, then fill in the gaps to complete her profile.

Captain Marvel's real name is Carol Danvers. While Carol was investigating an alien race called the Kree, an alien object exploded and added Kree DNA to her body. This event gave Carol many extraordinary powers.

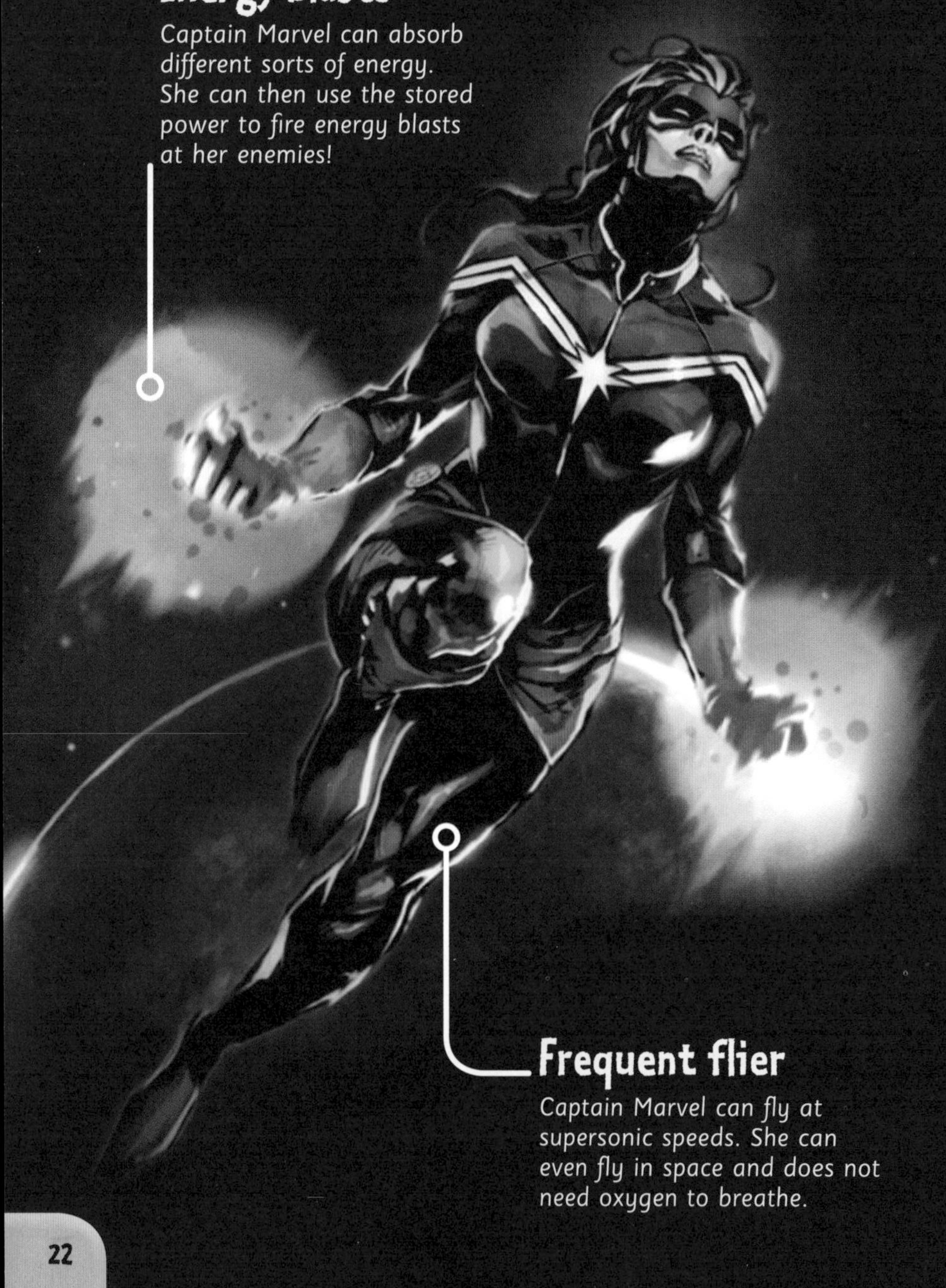

Energy blasts

Captain Marvel can absorb different sorts of energy. She can then use the stored power to fire energy blasts at her enemies!

Frequent flier

Captain Marvel can fly at supersonic speeds. She can even fly in space and does not need oxygen to breathe.

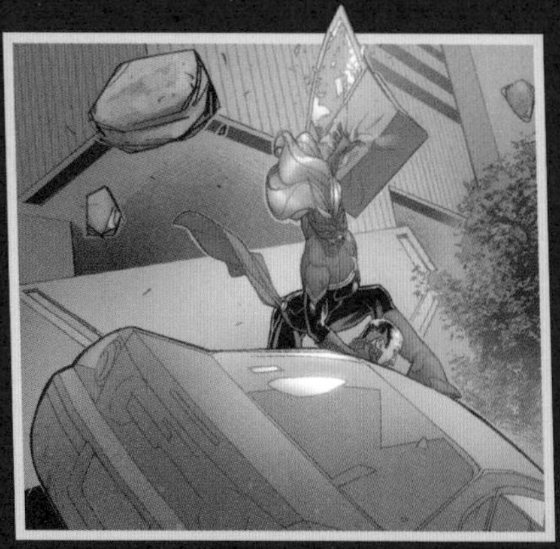

Packing a punch

Ripping off a car door is no problem for Captain Marvel because she is super-strong. She can increase her strength if she absorbs more energy.

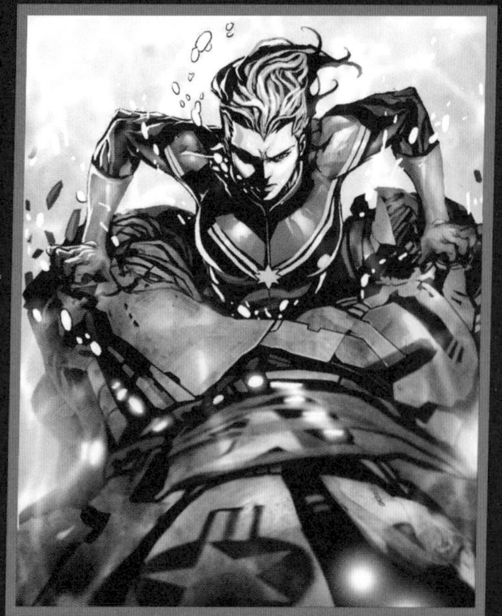

Tough as nails

Bullets cannot hurt Captain Marvel as her skin is super-tough. She is also highly resistant to poison or infections.

Find the **sticker** of Captain Marvel to complete the profile.

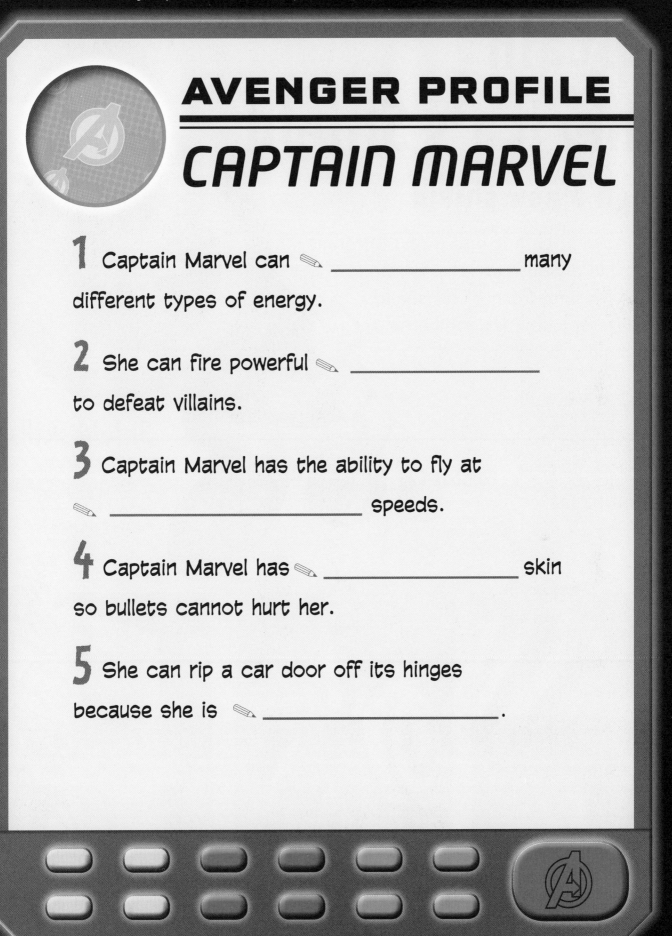

AVENGER PROFILE

CAPTAIN MARVEL

1 Captain Marvel can ✎ ________________ many different types of energy.

2 She can fire powerful ✎ ________________ to defeat villains.

3 Captain Marvel has the ability to fly at ✎ ________________ speeds.

4 Captain Marvel has ✎ ________________ skin so bullets cannot hurt her.

5 She can rip a car door off its hinges because she is ✎ ________________.

Find the **answers** on page 97.

Fact Challenge

Captain America's Shield

Design a new shield

Captain America has had many different shields. He always carries one into battle with him. Each of his shields have different abilities, which help him fight his many enemies.

Read about Captain America's different shields, then design a new one and write what it can do.

Stars and stripes

The shield is painted in the red, white, and blue of the American flag.

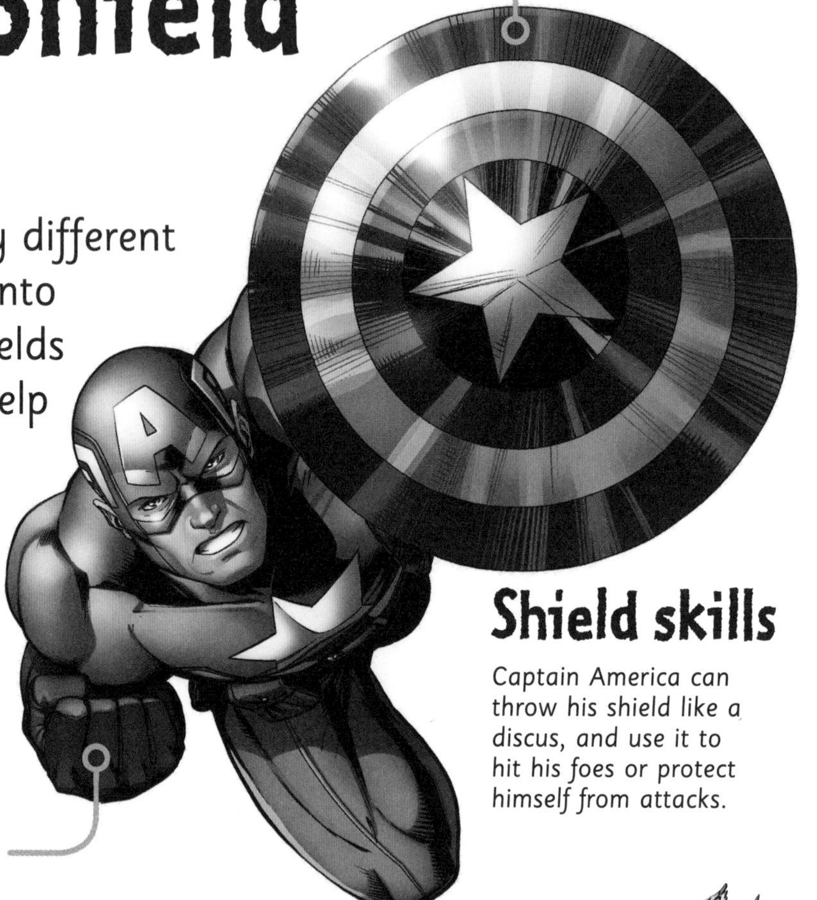

Combat Cap

Captain America is an expert fighter. He uses martial arts to defeat his foes.

Shield skills

Captain America can throw his shield like a discus, and use it to hit his foes or protect himself from attacks.

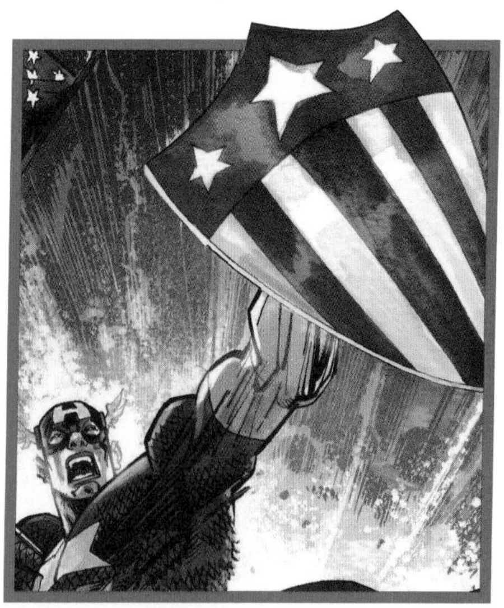

Original shield

Captain America used his first, bulletproof shield in World War II. He eventually replaced it with his more famous, circular shield.

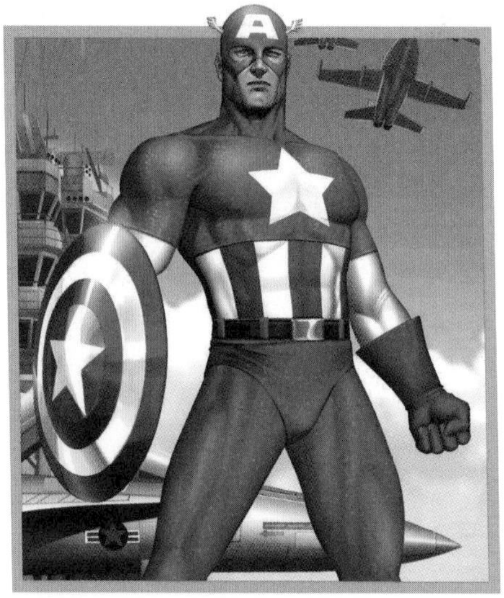

Vibranium shield

This circular shield is made out of Vibranium, a mysterious metal. It is really strong, and becomes even tougher as it absorbs more energy.

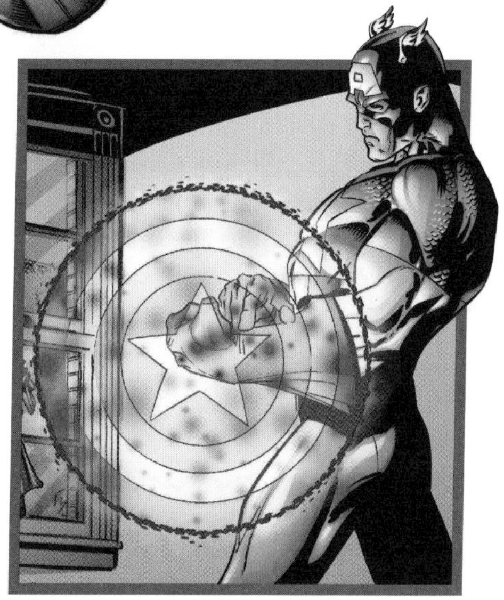

Energy shield

This shield is made out of energy and can fire energy blasts. It can also expand to protect his entire body or turn into a sword.

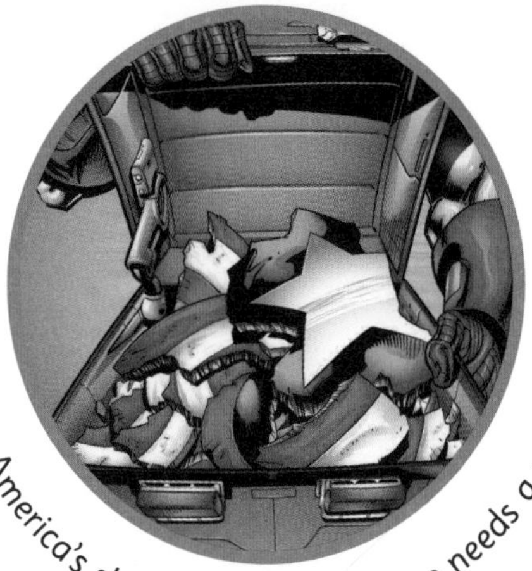

Captain America's shield has broken, so he needs a new one!

My new shield can:

The star spin's
it turns sharp
The midle star comes out
to be a throwing star

Your shield could have **built-in weapons**, like a laser gun.

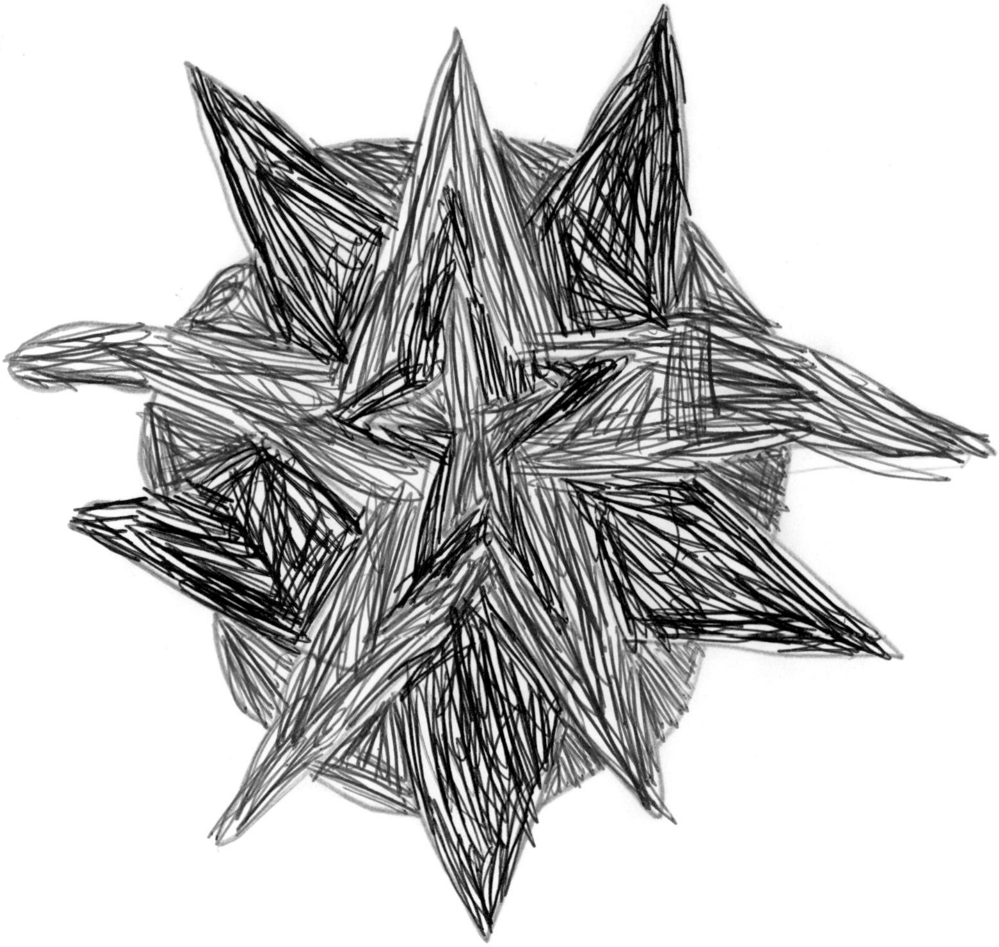

The new shield could be **a different shape**, like a rectangle or a star.

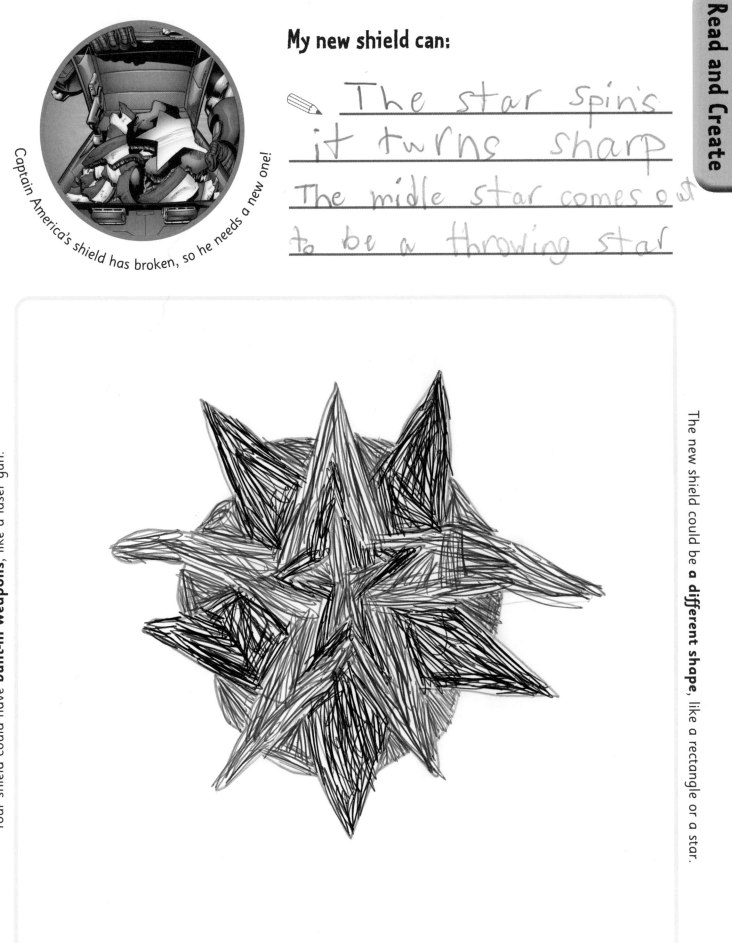

You could use **different colors**, like black and gold.

Hawkeye's Arrows

Choose the right arrow

Hawkeye is a master archer. His amazing accuracy makes him a vital member of the Avengers in any dangerous situation. His special trick arrows also make him a deadly opponent.

Read about some of Hawkeye's trick arrows, then choose which arrow to use in each situation.

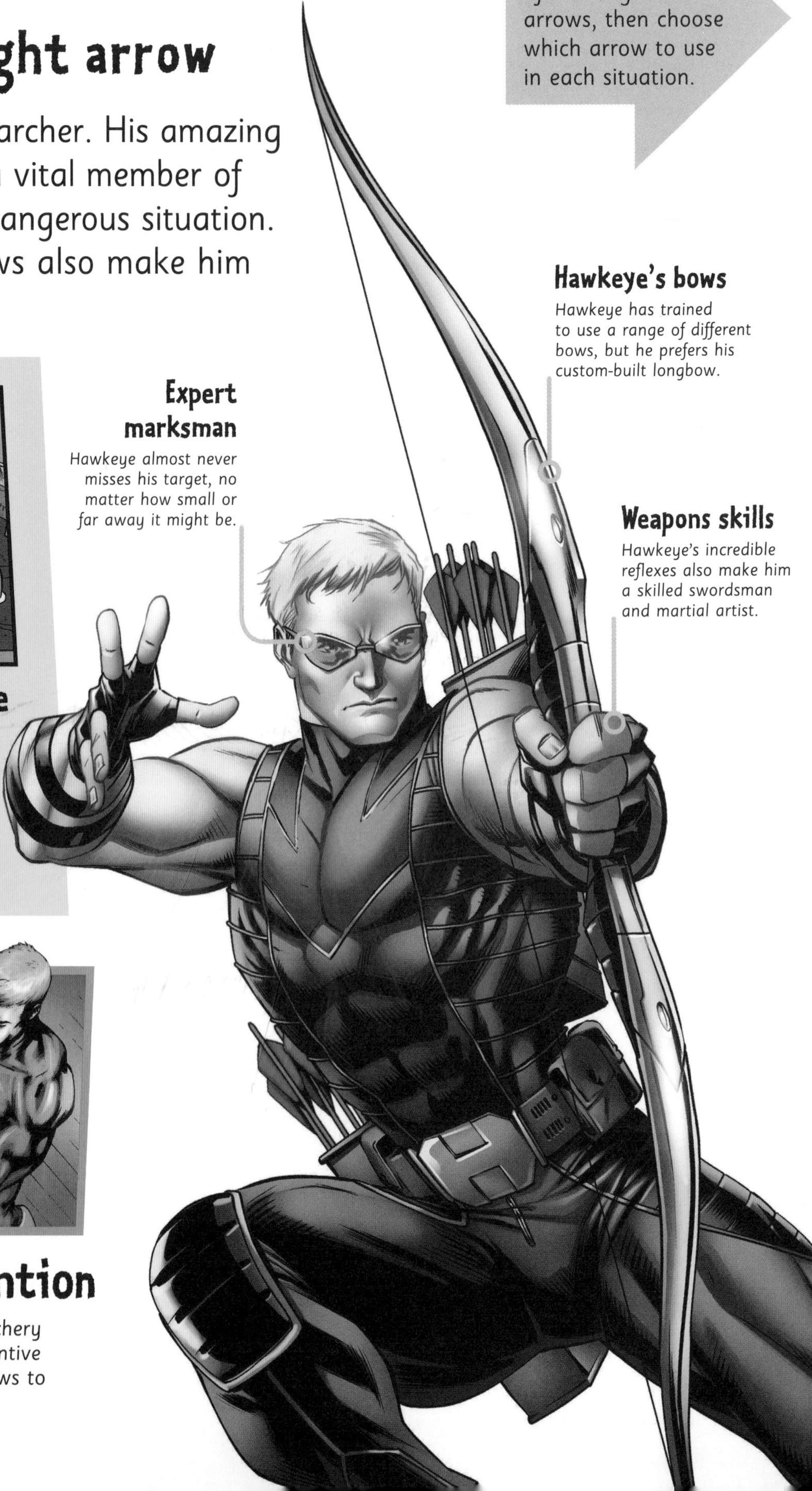

Hawkeye's bows

Hawkeye has trained to use a range of different bows, but he prefers his custom-built longbow.

Expert marksman

Hawkeye almost never misses his target, no matter how small or far away it might be.

Weapons skills

Hawkeye's incredible reflexes also make him a skilled swordsman and martial artist.

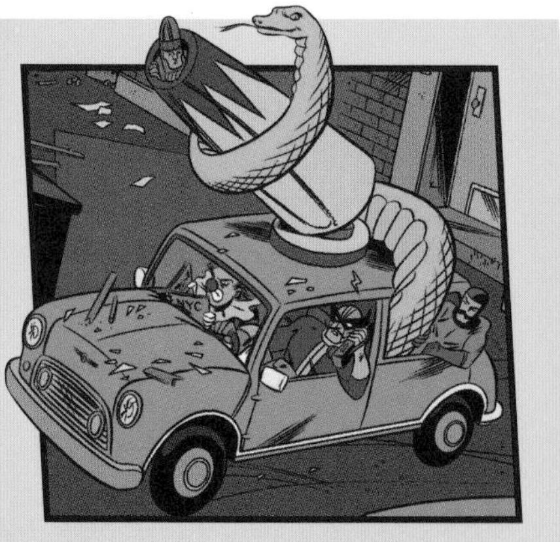

The Circus of Crime

When he was a boy, Hawkeye ran away to join the circus—it was here he learned his skills. The circus was actually a criminal enterprise run by the evil ringmaster Maynard Tibolt.

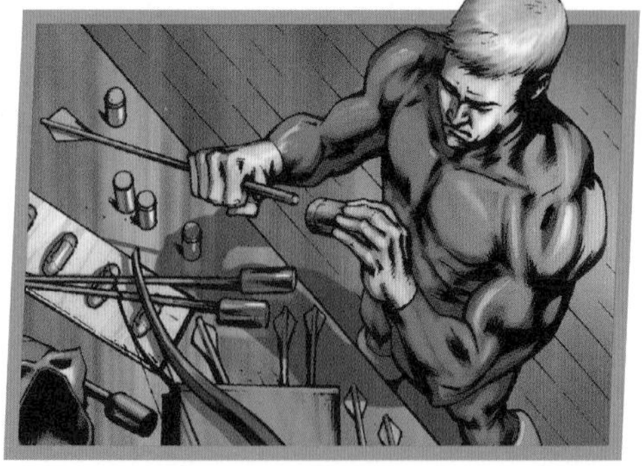

Master of invention

As well as his acrobatic and archery skills, Hawkeye has a keen inventive mind. He has created trick arrows to deal with nearly any situation.

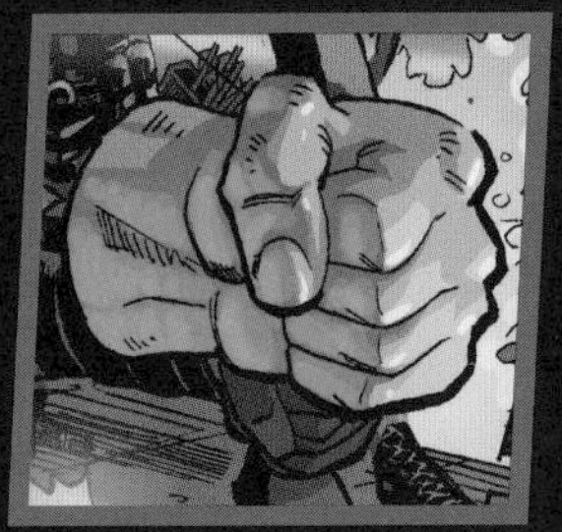

Hulk punch arrow

Hawkeye borrowed this arrow from his ally Deadpool. The fist looks like a toy, but is actually full of powerful explosives.

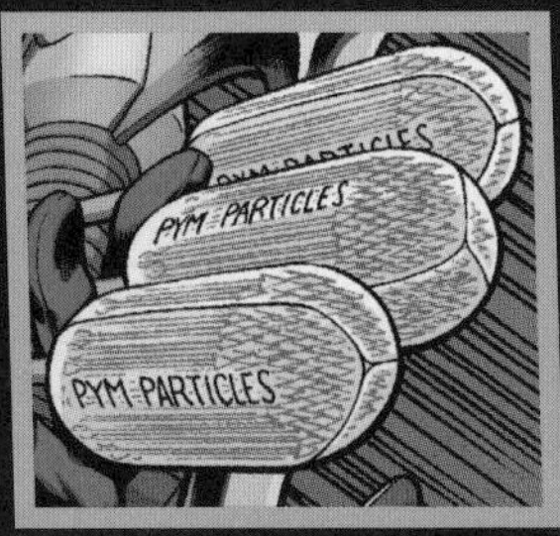
PYM PARTICLES
PYM PARTICLES
PYM PARTICLES

Cluster arrow

This arrow is packed with growth particles and tiny darts. When it explodes, the darts grow bigger and shower the entire area.

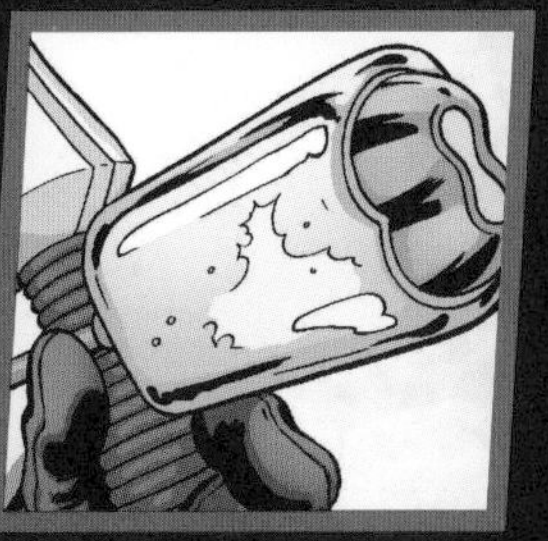

Freeze arrow

Anything hit by this arrow will instantly freeze solid, whether it is a person, a vehicle, or a complex piece of machinery.

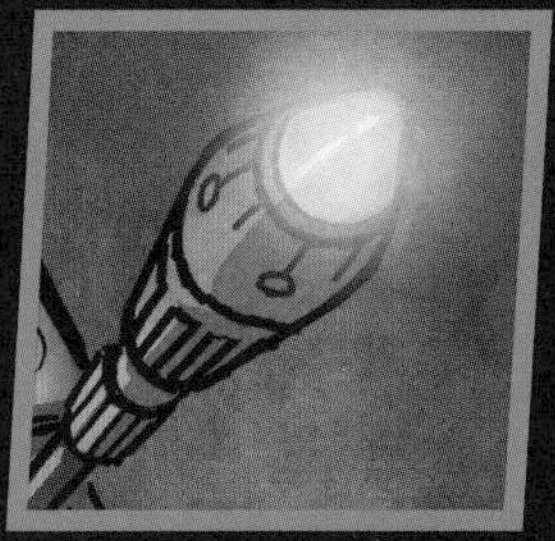

Portal arrow

This high-tech arrow can make solid walls disappear, allowing Hawkeye to easily escape from dead ends or locked rooms.

Find the **stickers** at the back of the book.

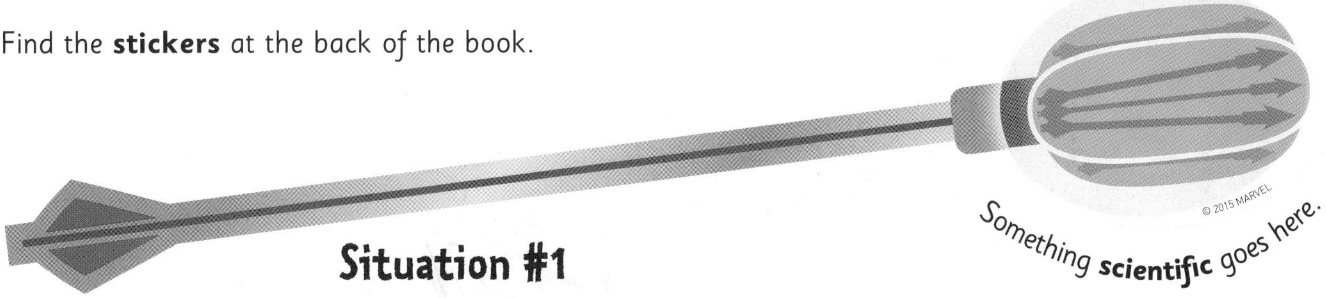
© 2015 MARVEL
Something **scientific** goes here.

Situation #1

A crowd of mobsters is shooting at Hawkeye. Which arrow could take them all out at once?

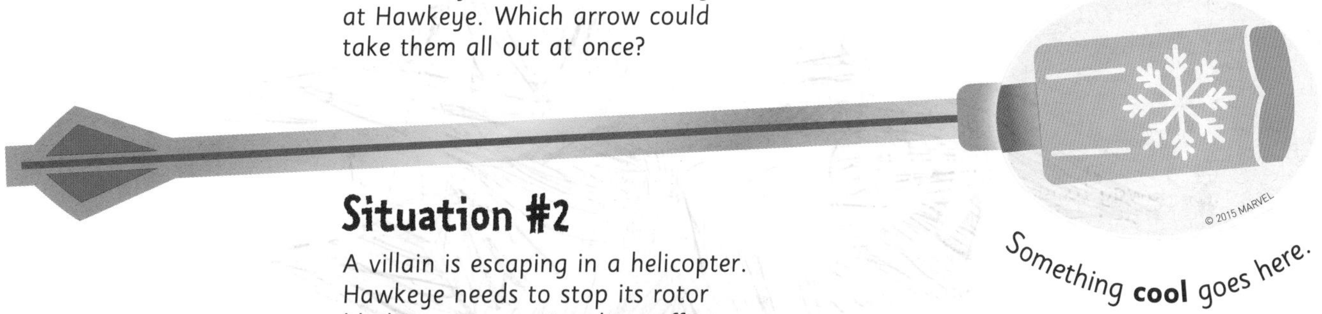
© 2015 MARVEL
Something **cool** goes here.

Situation #2

A villain is escaping in a helicopter. Hawkeye needs to stop its rotor blades to prevent it taking off!

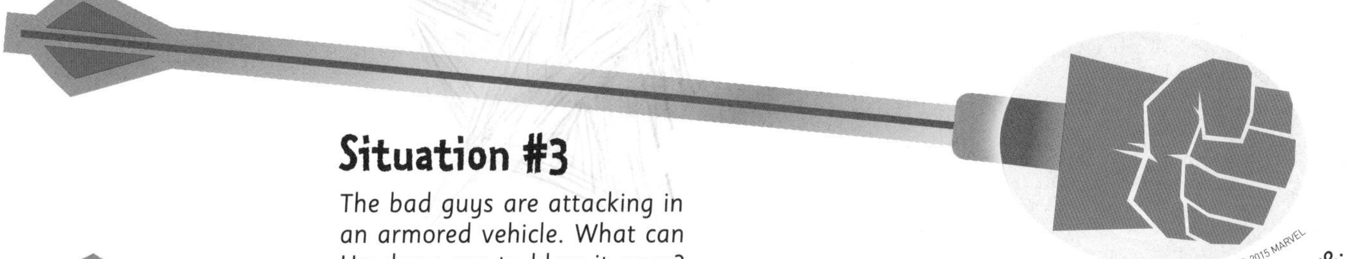
© 2015 MARVEL
Something **powerful** goes here.

Situation #3

The bad guys are attacking in an armored vehicle. What can Hawkeye use to blow it open?

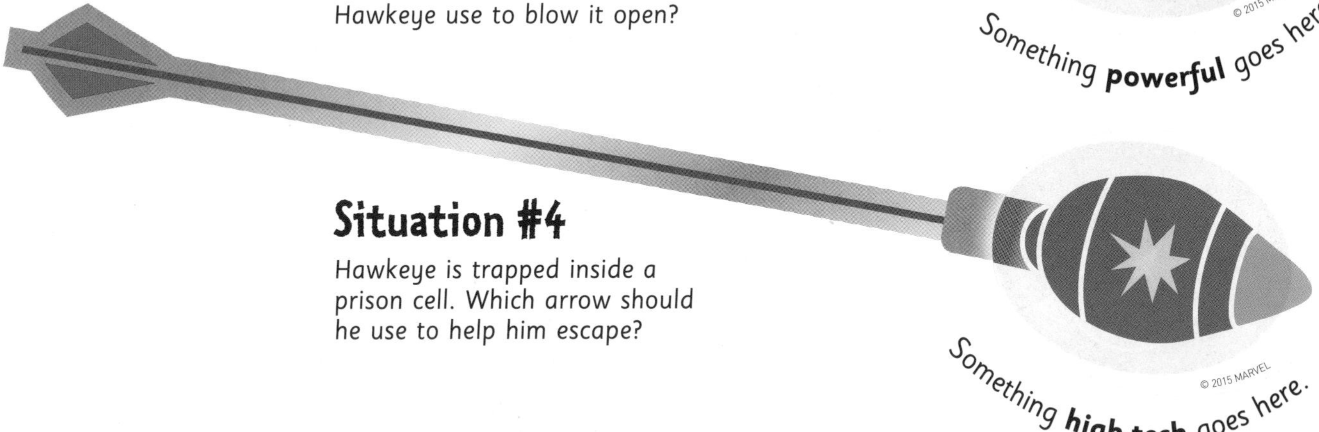
© 2015 MARVEL
Something **high-tech** goes here.

Situation #4

Hawkeye is trapped inside a prison cell. Which arrow should he use to help him escape?

Find the **answers** on page 97.

Black Widow

Invent a new gadget

Black Widow is one of the world's greatest spies. She is a skilled acrobat, and her powerful combat techniques and futuristic spy gear means that no mission is ever too difficult!

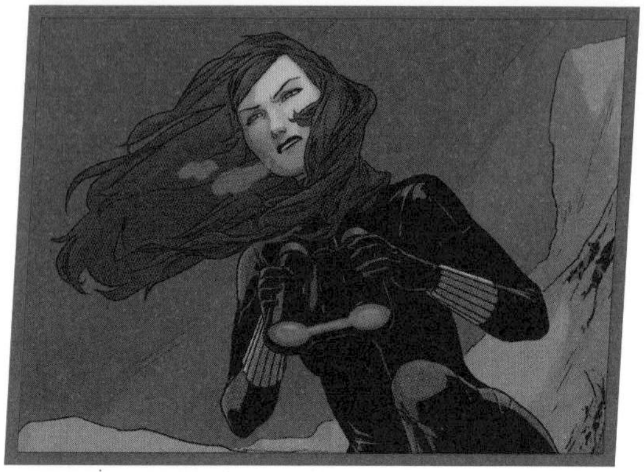

Super-spy

Black Widow was given the Super-Soldier Serum, which granted her super-strength, speed, agility, and toughness. It has also slowed the aging process—she is actually over 70 years old!

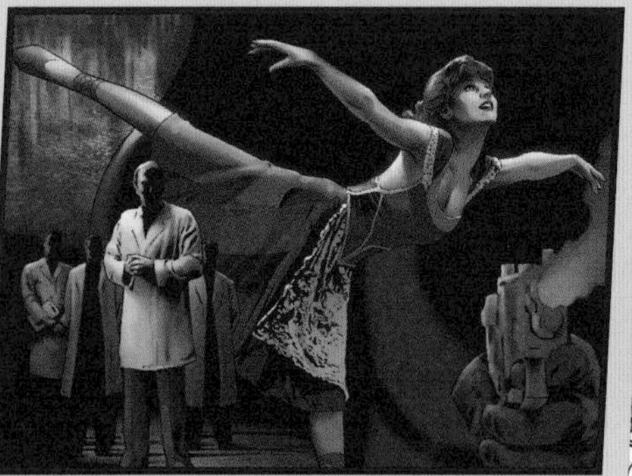

Mysterious origins

Black Widow's real name is Natalia Romanova. She grew up in Russia during World War II, and later became one of Russia's top spies. For a time, she worked undercover as a ballerina in the famous Bolshoi Theater.

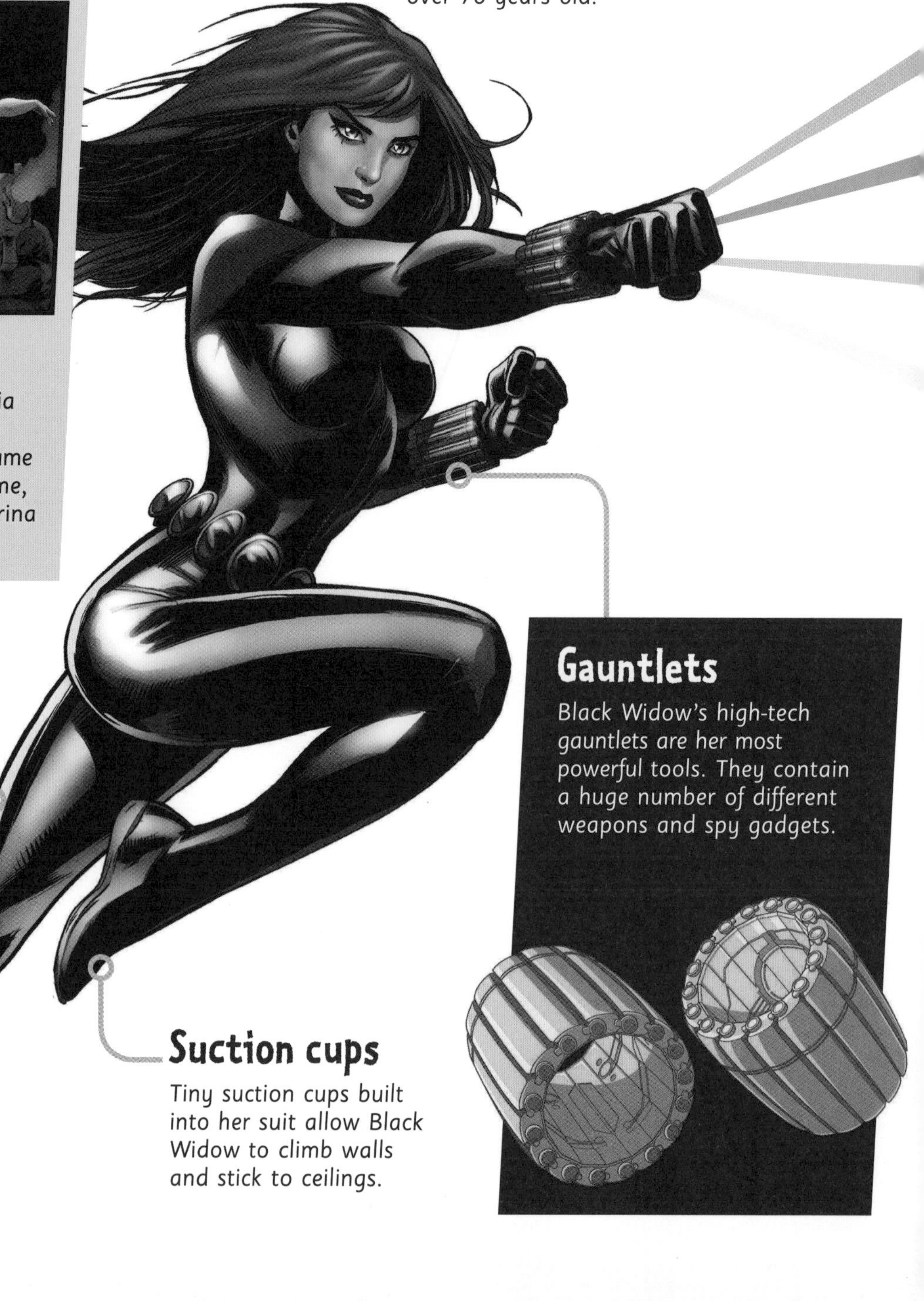

Spy suit

This special stretchy fabric suit is designed to be both bulletproof and heat-resistant.

Suction cups

Tiny suction cups built into her suit allow Black Widow to climb walls and stick to ceilings.

Gauntlets

Black Widow's high-tech gauntlets are her most powerful tools. They contain a huge number of different weapons and spy gadgets.

Find the **stickers** at the back of the book.

Find the stickers of Black Widow's gadgets, then invent a new one for her.

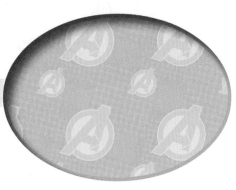

Widow's Bite

The Widow's Bite is Black Widow's deadliest weapon. It fires blasts of high-voltage electricity at her targets. The Widow's Bite can also be used to stun people.

Widow's Kiss

The Widow's Kiss is a powerful knock-out drug. It looks like a pinkish mist, and just a few breaths is enough to make someone unconscious for hours.

Widow's Line

For the Widow's Line, the gauntlets fire out a strong cable. Black Widow can then use it to climb up things, or swing from place to place.

What is your gadget **used for**?

Give your gadget a **name**.

Widow's ______________________

The Quinjet

Complete the sticker jigsaw

The Quinjet is the Avengers' team shuttle. It flies at twice the speed of sound, can take off or land without a runway, and carries the heroes into battle anywhere on Earth (and beyond).

Use the sticker pieces to put the Quinjet together.

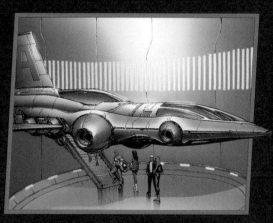

Preparing for battle

The Quinjet's spacious cockpit is a good place for the Avengers to discuss their battle plans. They can also review any information on their enemy, as they fly to the site of trouble.

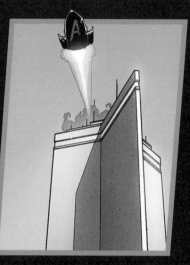

Stark Tower base

When Stark Tower became the Avengers' new home, the Quinjet moved with them. It is based in a hangar at the top of the skyscraper.

Quinjet prototypes

There have been many different Quinjets over the years. Tony Stark (AKA Iron Man) recently built a new, advanced Quinjet, but like many others it was destroyed shortly afterward.

Into the blue

The Quinjet doesn't just fly—it can also transport the Avengers far into outer space, or deep into the darkest depths of the oceans.

Find the **stickers** at the back of the book.

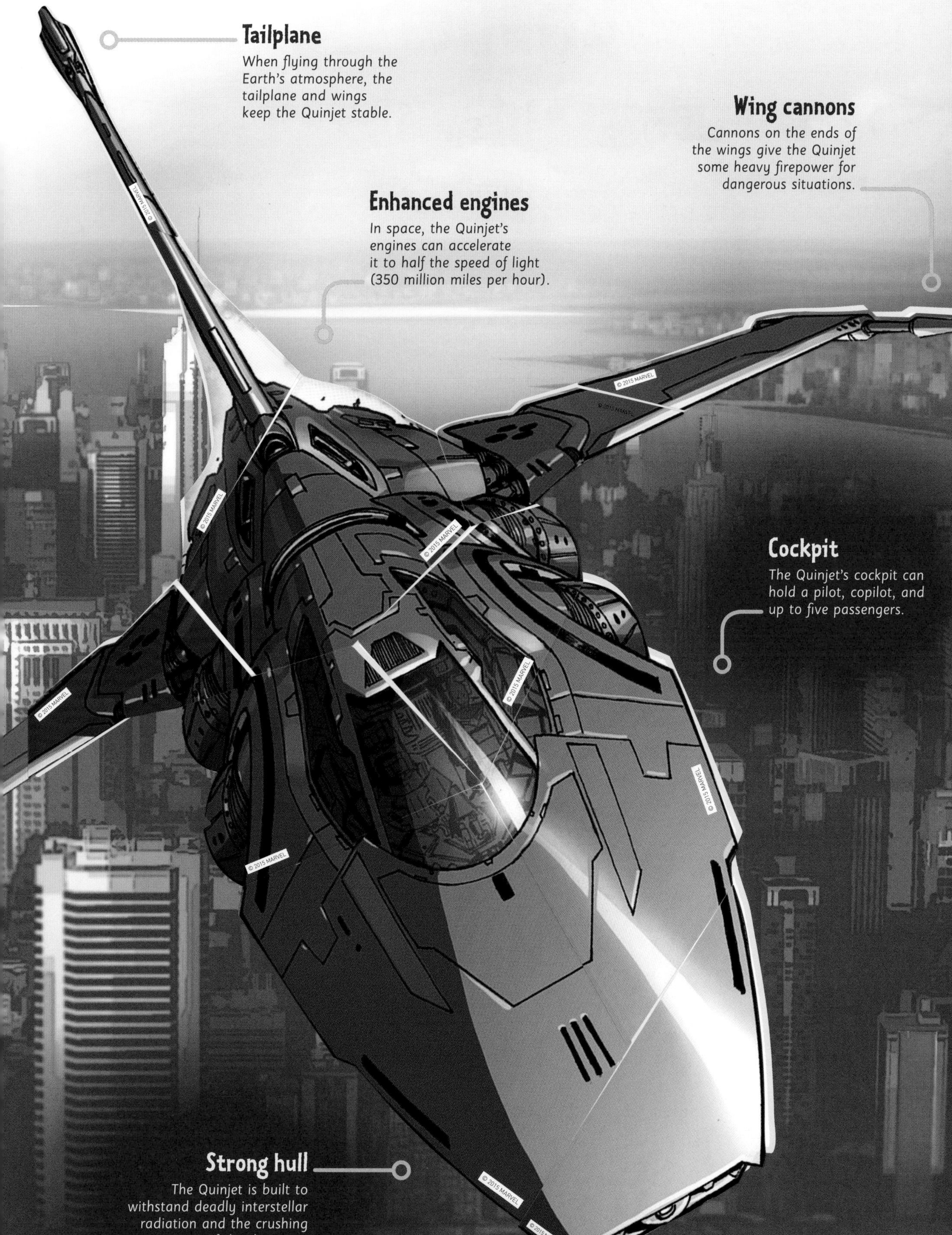

Tailplane
When flying through the Earth's atmosphere, the tailplane and wings keep the Quinjet stable.
Wing cannons
Cannons on the ends of the wings give the Quinjet some heavy firepower for dangerous situations.
Enhanced engines
In space, the Quinjet's engines can accelerate it to half the speed of light (350 million miles per hour).
Cockpit
The Quinjet's cockpit can hold a pilot, copilot, and up to five passengers.
Strong hull
The Quinjet is built to withstand deadly interstellar radiation and the crushing pressures of the deep sea.

Chapter 2 Challenge

Test your knowledge of this chapter

Answer each question. If you need help, look back through the section.

Now you have finished the second chapter of the book, take the Challenge to prove your knowledge!

1. Find the sticker that best matches the description:

This golden spear symbolizes Odin's power and is made from enchanted metal.

2. The Quinjet's cockpit can carry a pilot, copilot, and up to how many passengers?

Four ☐ **Seven** ☐ **Five** ☐

3. Captain Marvel does not need oxygen to breathe in space.

True ☐ **False** ☐

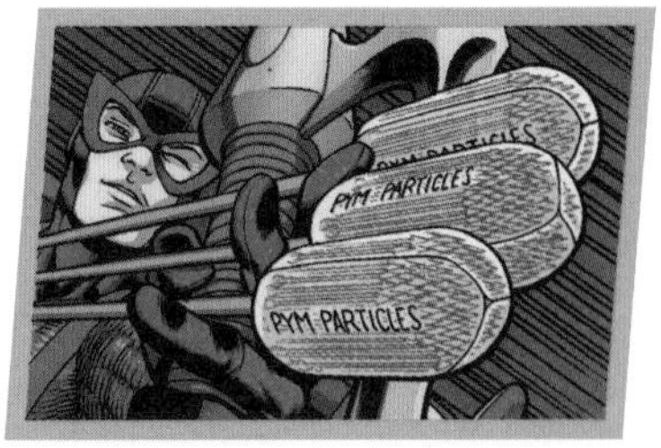
PYM PARTICLES
PYM PARTICLES
PYM PARTICLES

4. What is the name of Hawkeye's trick weapon that contains growth particles?

✎ ______________________________

5. Black Widow's ✎ ____________________ are her most powerful tools. They hold lots of gadgets and weapons.

Find the **answers** on page 97.

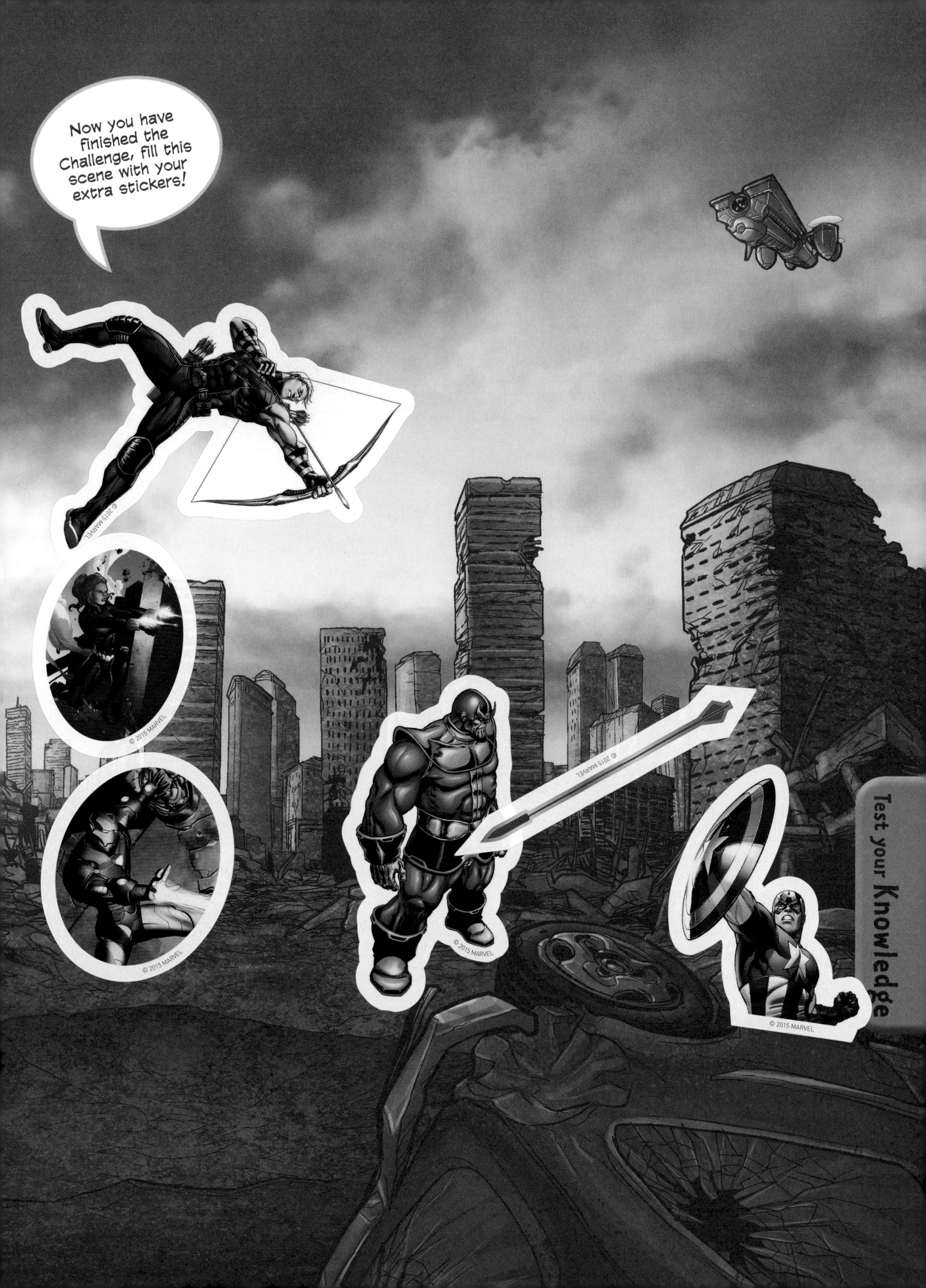
Now you have finished the Challenge, fill this scene with your extra stickers!
© 2015 MARVEL
© 2015 MARVEL
© 2015 MARVEL
© 2015 MARVEL
© 2015 MARVEL
© 2015 MARVEL
© 2015 MARVEL

CHAPTER 3 [redacted]

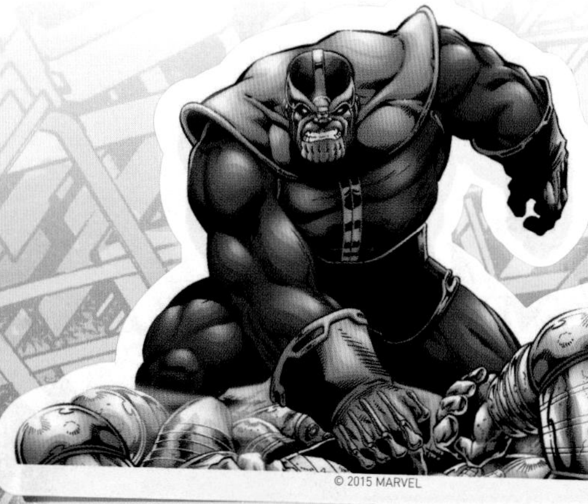
© 2015 MARVEL

Thanos

Thanos is a terrifying, evil alien who has destroyed many worlds across the galaxy. He possesses superhuman levels of toughness and strength.

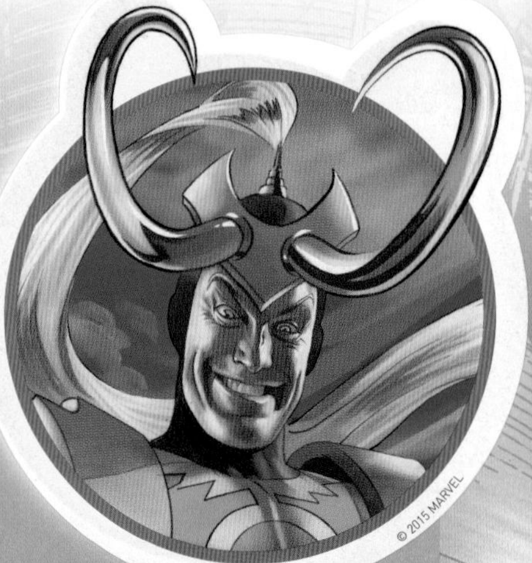
© 2015 MARVEL

Loki

Loki is a powerful enemy of both Thor and the Avengers. He betrayed his own family in an attempt to take over the realm of Asgard.

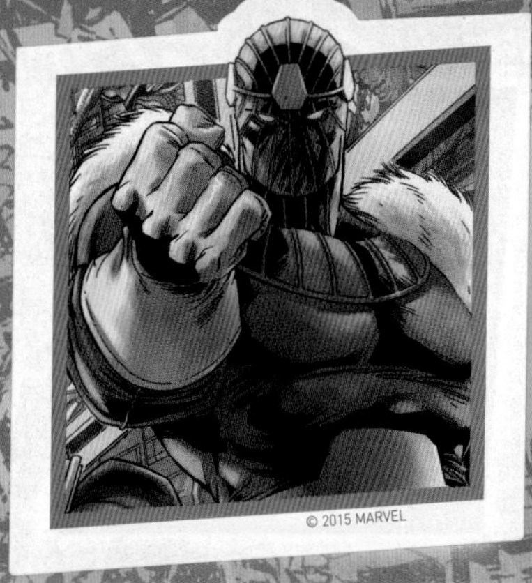
© 2015 MARVEL

Baron Zemo

Baron Zemo is an archenemy of the Avengers. He is an excellent fighter and commander, and often leads the Masters of Evil.

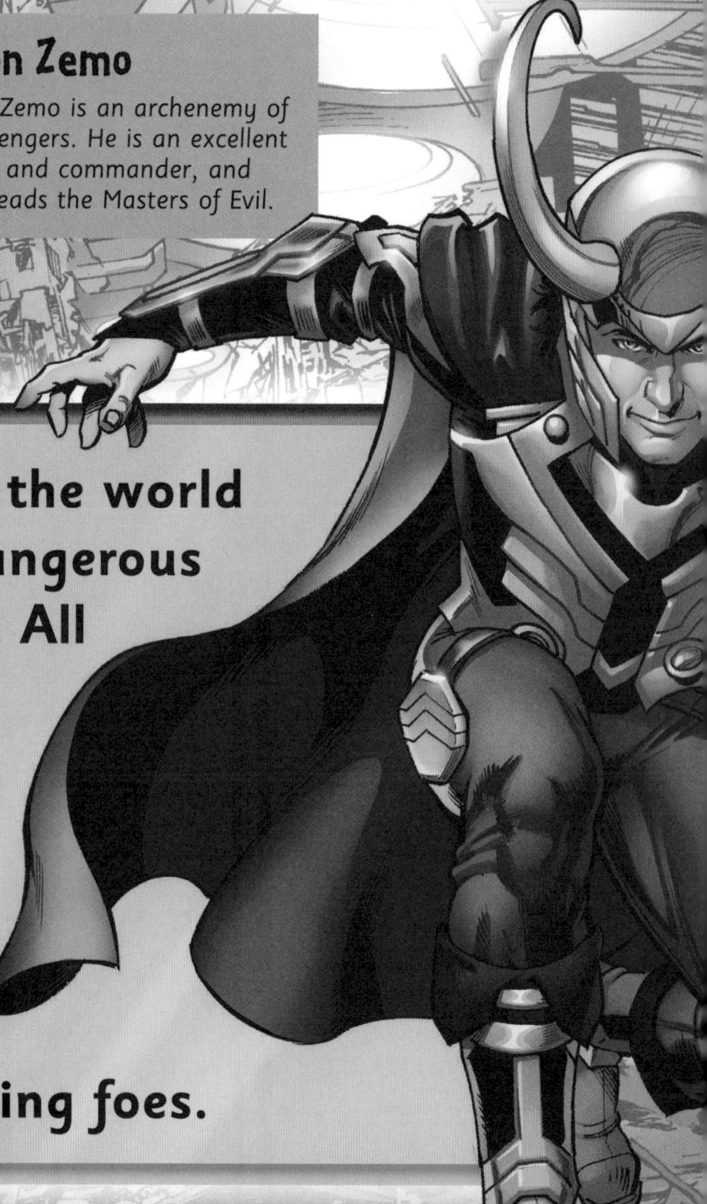

The Avengers protect the world from powerful and dangerous super-human enemies. All of these villains have incredible abilities that they use for evil. Luckily, Earth's Mightiest Heroes are always prepared to battle these terrifying foes.

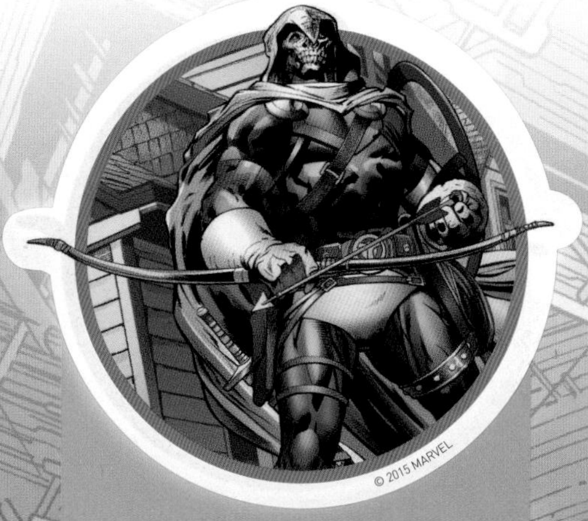
© 2015 MARVEL

Taskmaster

The fearsome Taskmaster's real name is Tony Masters. He is a superb fighter and has memorized many different fighting techniques. This makes him a deadly opponent.

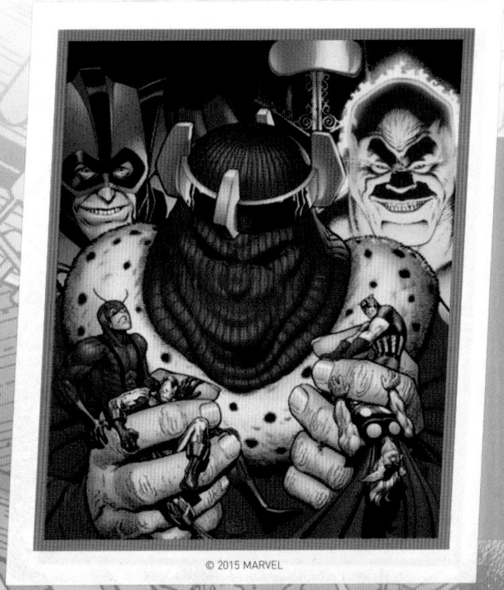
© 2015 MARVEL

The Masters of Evil

The Masters of Evil are a dangerous group of Super Villains that often battles the Avengers. They even destroyed the Avengers Mansion!

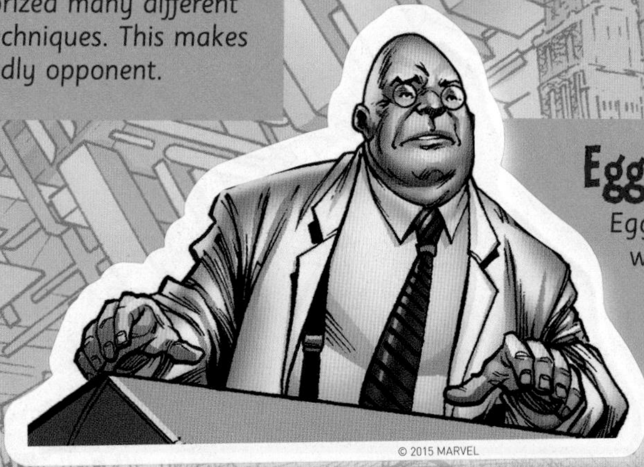
© 2015 MARVEL

Egghead

Egghead is an evil scientist, whose real name is Elihas Starr. He once worked for the US government, but now he lives a life of crime.

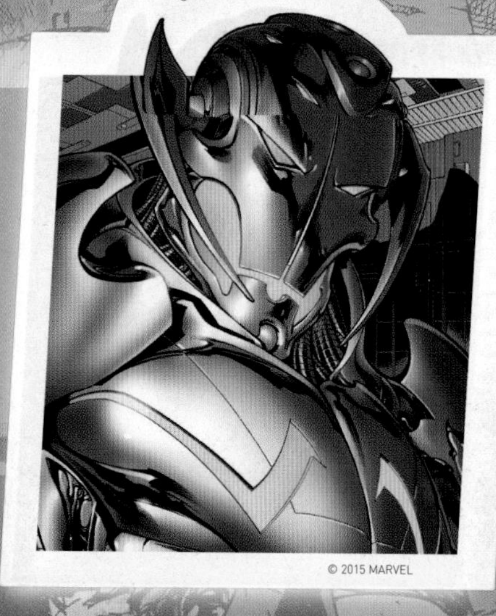
© 2015 MARVEL

Ultron

This evil robot wants to rule the world—and he has nearly succeeded on many occasions! Ultron has super-strong armor that is practically indestructible.

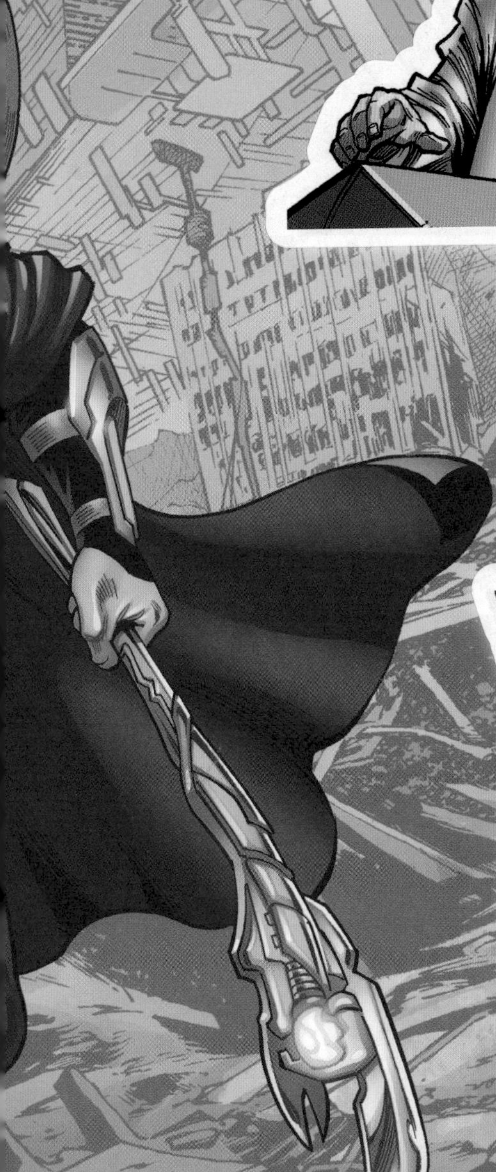

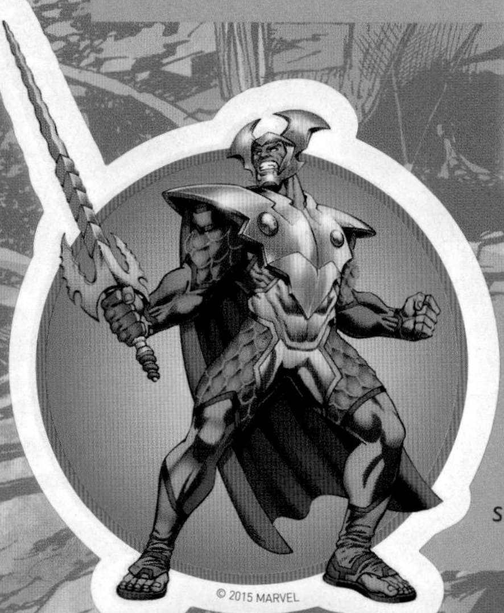
© 2015 MARVEL

Attuma

Attuma is a powerful warrior who believes it is his right to rule the underwater world of Atlantis. He is very strong and has superhuman reflexes.

Loki Laufeyson

Create a Wanted poster

Loki is the god of mischief, and Thor's adopted brother. Growing up, Loki became jealous of Thor's strength and bravery. He decided to use magic to destroy Thor and take over their home kingdom of Asgard.

Learn about Loki, then complete the Wanted poster opposite.

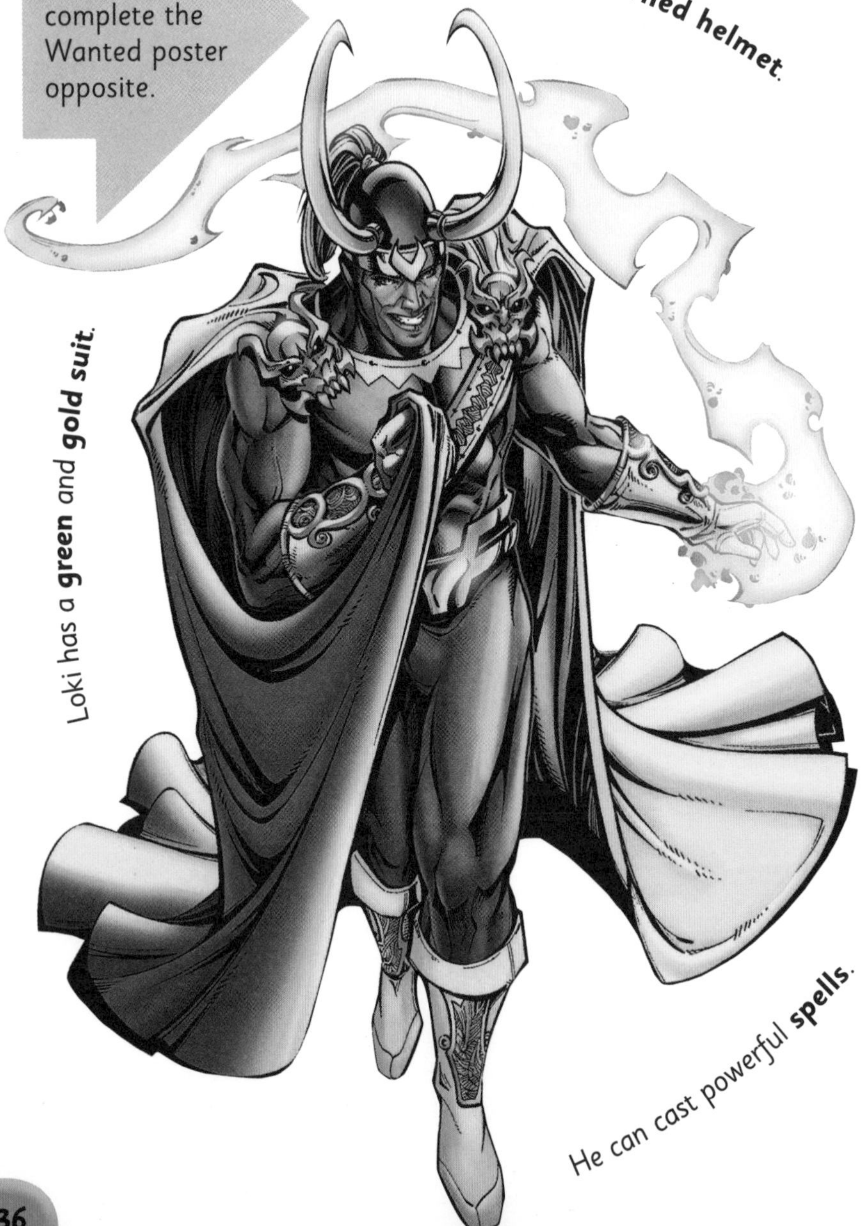

Loki wears a **horned helmet.**
Loki has a **green** and **gold suit.**
He can cast powerful **spells.**

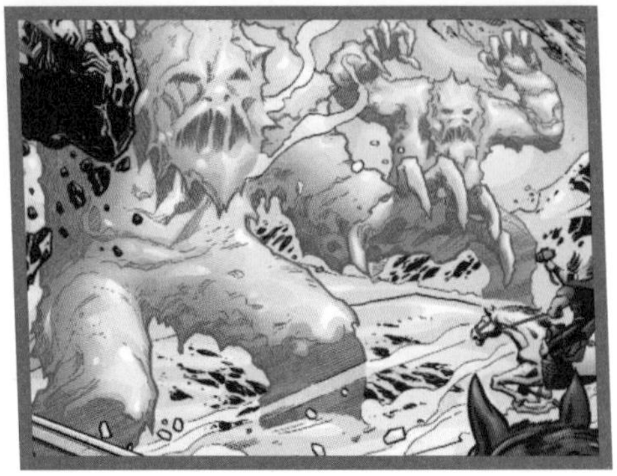

Son of Frost Giants

Loki is really the son of Laufey, king of the Frost Giants of Jotunheim, and sworn enemy of Asgard. After defeating Laufey, Thor's father Odin took Loki in and raised him as his own son.

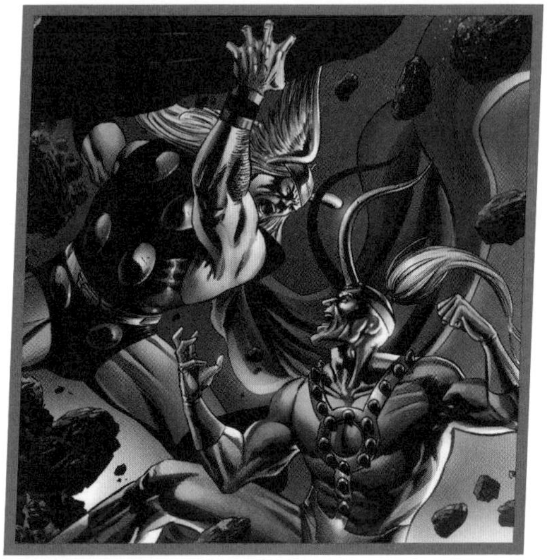

Brotherly love...

Loki and Thor could not be more different. Thor uses his strength in battle, but Loki fights using deceit, lies, and magic.

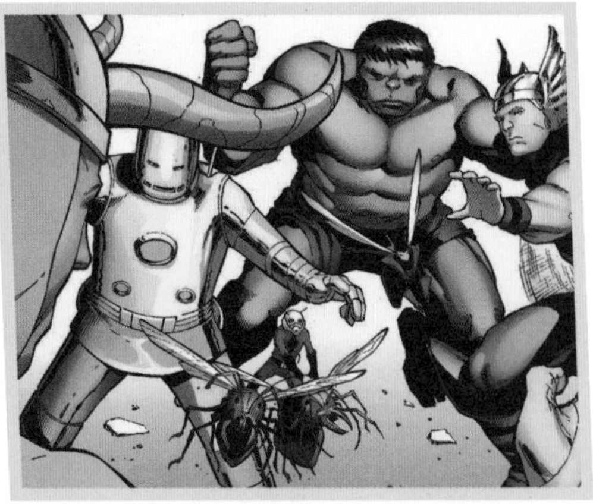

Loki versus the Avengers

Loki was the first enemy that the Avengers ever faced. By working together, they were able to defeat him!

WANTED: LOKI
FOR CRIMES AGAINST ASGARD AND THE EARTH!

Make sure you draw Loki's **costume**.

Draw **Loki** on the poster.

Loki, god of ✏️_____ and son of the Frost

Giant king ✏️_____ has escaped! Thor has

gathered Earth's Mightiest Heroes, the ✏️_____

to defeat him. Loki wears a green and ✏️_____ suit

and a horned ✏️_____ . His weapons are lies, deceit,

and ✏️_____ . **BEWARE!**

Fill in the **missing words**.

Find the **answers** on page 97.

Evil Villains

Identify the Super Villains

The Avengers have faced some strange and mysterious enemies. Some villains want power or revenge, while others like to destroy things simply because they can.

Read about these villains, then use the clues to identify them.

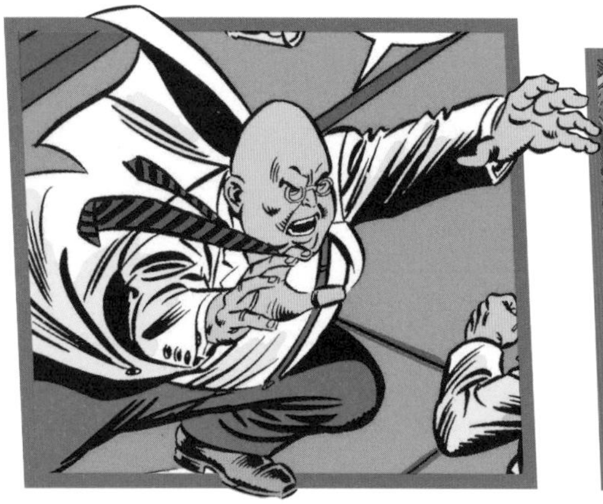

Egghead

Egghead's real name is Elihas Starr. This evil genius was arrested for betraying the United States, and then decided to become a master criminal.

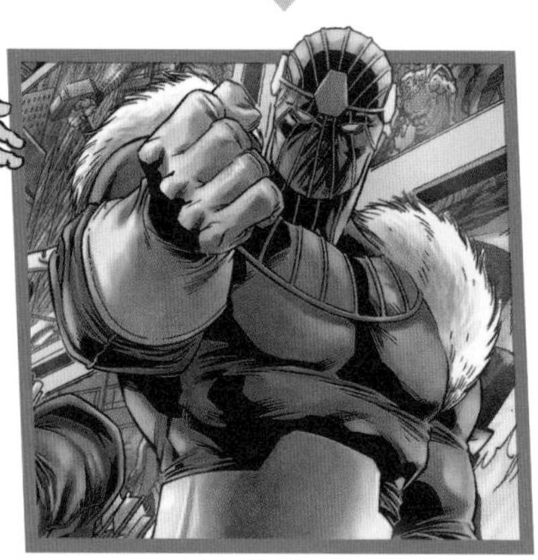

Baron Zemo

Heinrich Zemo was one of the smartest scientists in Nazi Germany. His hood became permanently stuck to his head in an accident, which drove him insane.

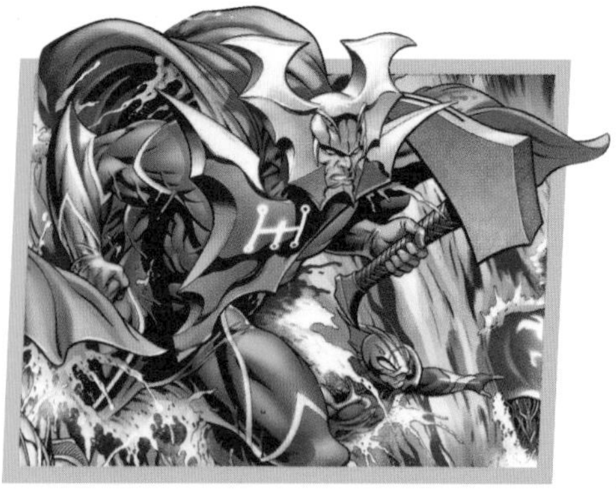

Attuma

Attuma comes from an undersea barbarian tribe of Atlanteans. He has superhuman strength, but must stay near water or he will lose his powers.

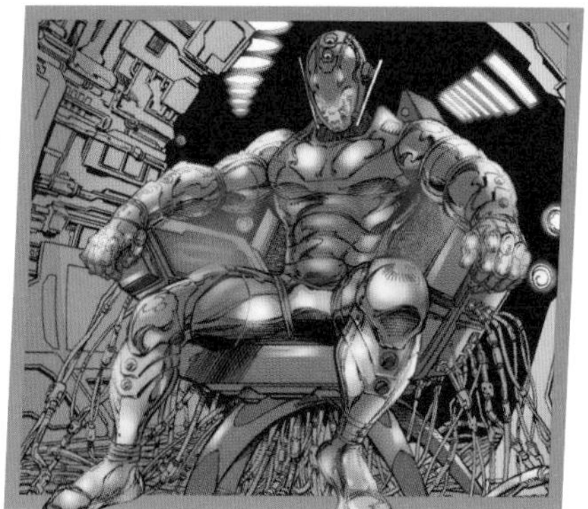

Ultron

Ultron is an evil robot built by the genius Dr. Hank Pym. Ultron rebelled against his creator and went on a terrifying rampage.

I was a scientist.

My face is hidden.

I wear purple.

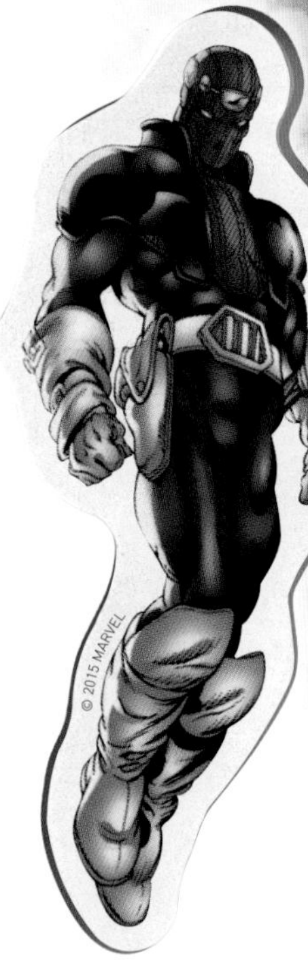

© 2015 MARVEL

1 My name is:

Baron Zemo

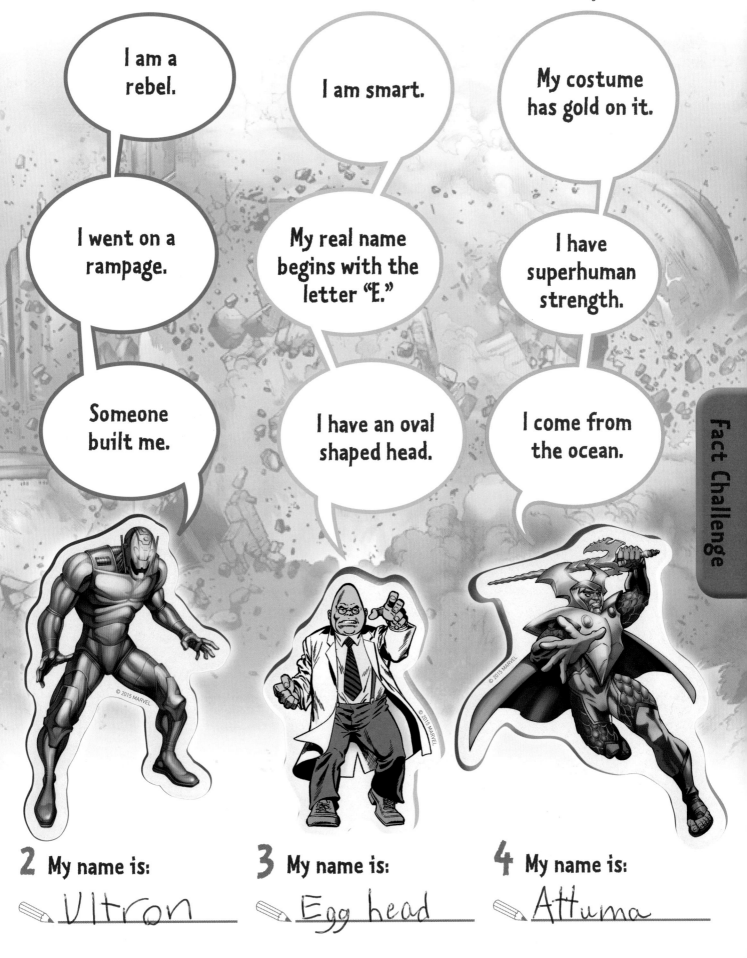

I am a rebel.

I went on a rampage.

Someone built me.

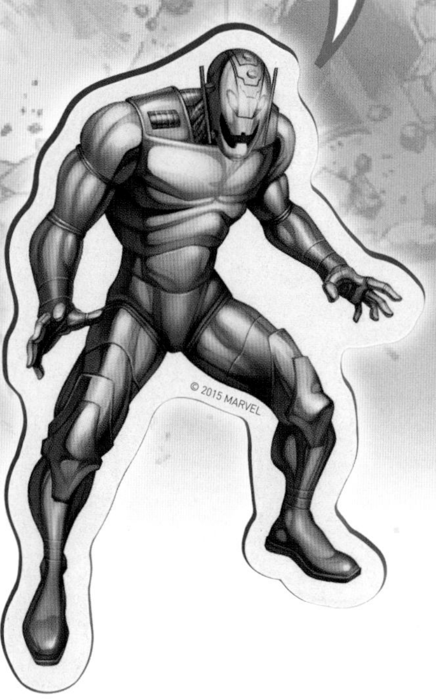
© 2015 MARVEL

I am smart.

My real name begins with the letter "E."

I have an oval shaped head.

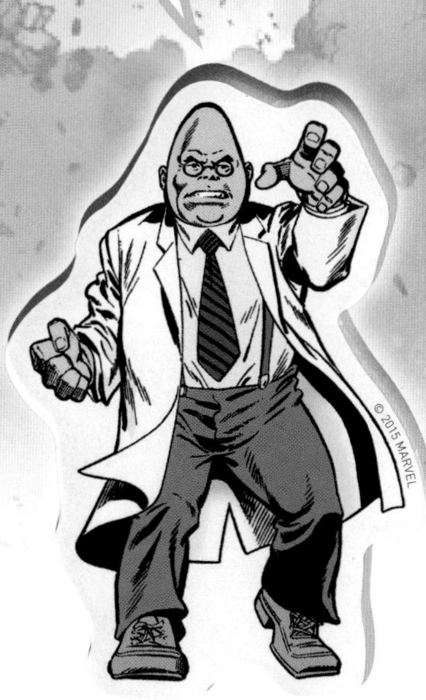
© 2015 MARVEL

My costume has gold on it.

I have superhuman strength.

I come from the ocean.

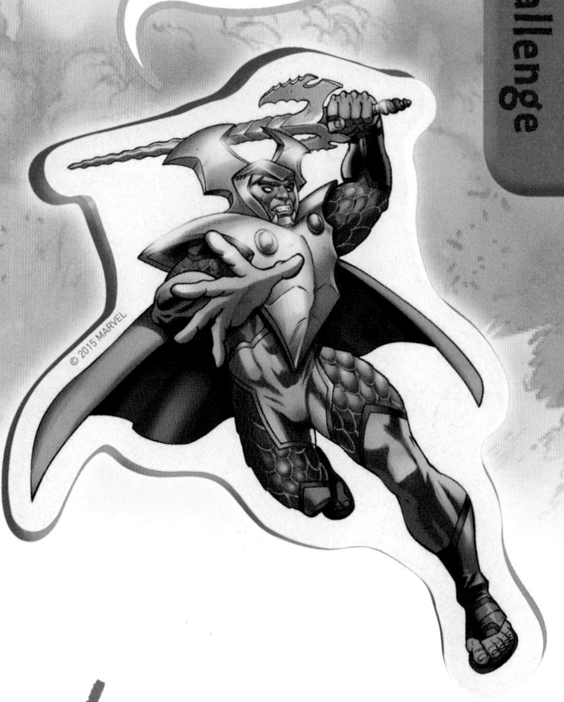
© 2015 MARVEL

2 My name is:

Ultron

3 My name is:

Egg head

4 My name is:

Attuma

Find the **answers** on page 97.

A New Enemy

Create a new Super Villain

The Avengers team was formed to fight the most powerful villains that no Super Hero could handle alone. The Avengers' greatest foes are smart and ruthless, and have powers that are both terrifying and destructive.

Read about these enemies of the Avengers, then design a new one.

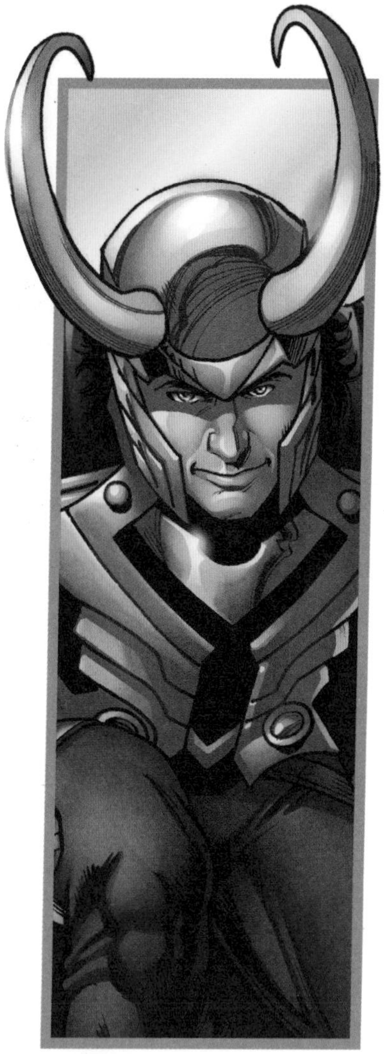

Loki

Loki has superhuman strength and toughness. He can also change shape, cast spells, and communicate with others using his mind.

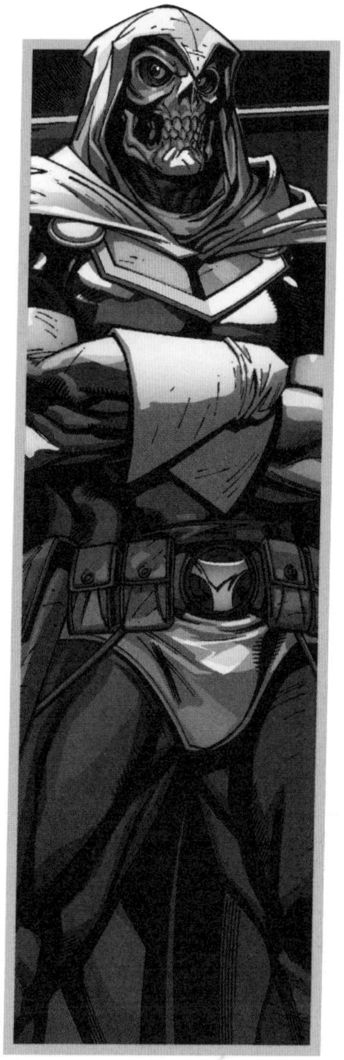

Taskmaster

Taskmaster is an expert in all types of combat. He has photographic reflexes, which means he can instantly copy anyone he battles.

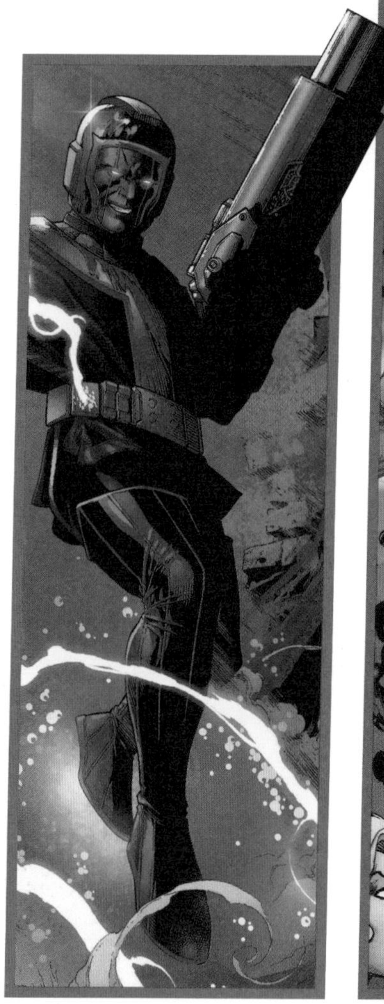

Kang

Kang likes to call himself "the Conqueror." This genius from the future wears powerful armor and carries futuristic weapons.

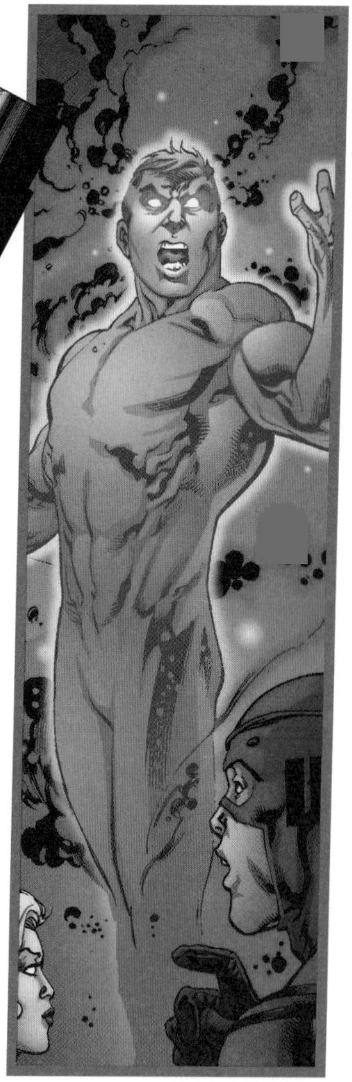

Korvac

Korvac is a god-like being from another dimension. He can travel through time and space, and even destroy the universe!

The Avengers' new enemy is called:

✏ <u>Elamental</u>

List the special powers your new villain has:

✏ <u>Super strengh</u>
<u>Huy Intelagents</u>
<u>turning into any</u>
<u>surphise</u>

Will your new villain wear **armor** or carry any special **equipment**?

What **abilities** does your villain have? Do they use **weapons** or special **powers**?

Make sure your villain looks really **scary**!

Thanos

Color in the villain

Thanos is a terrifying space pirate who is feared throughout the galaxy. Also known as the Mad Titan, Thanos has caused devastation in his never-ending quest to gain more power.

Dark intelligence

Thanos is a scientific genius. His knowledge has allowed him to create super-advanced and destructive technology.

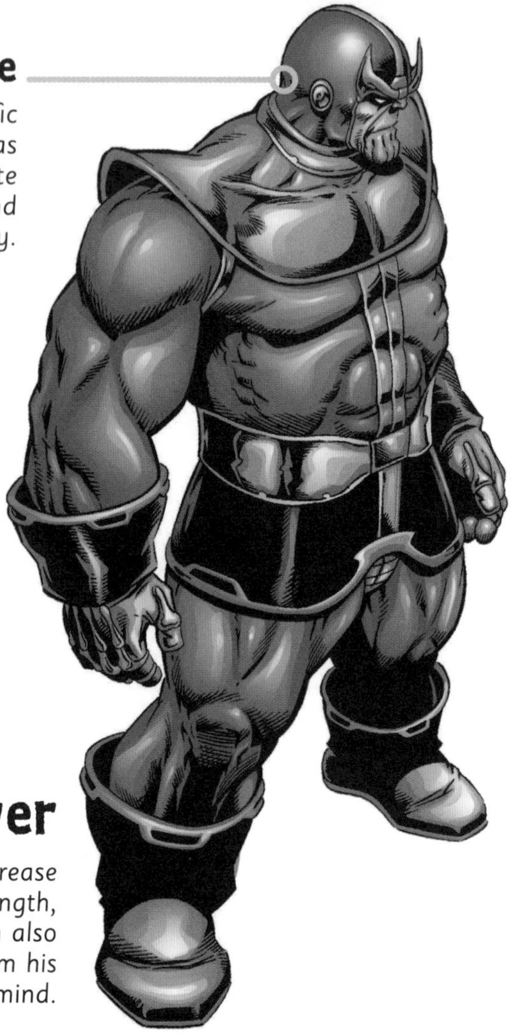

Read about Thanos and the Infinity Gauntlet, then color Thanos's other half.

Incredible power

Thanos can absorb energy to increase his superhuman levels of strength, toughness, and speed. He can also project powerful energy blasts from his hands and his mind.

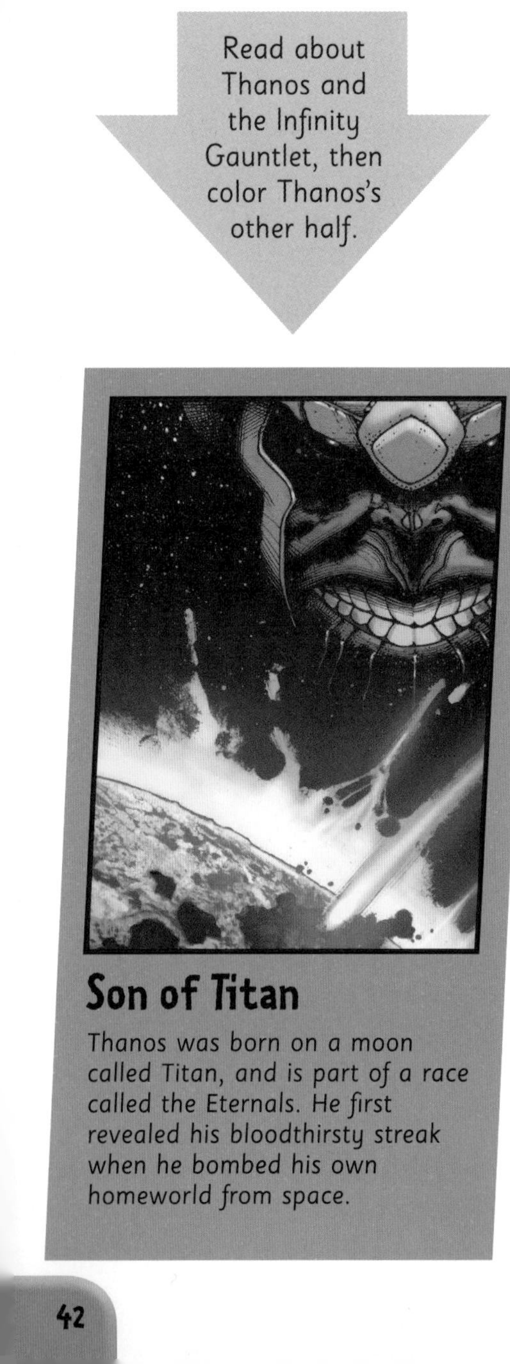

Son of Titan

Thanos was born on a moon called Titan, and is part of a race called the Eternals. He first revealed his bloodthirsty streak when he bombed his own homeworld from space.

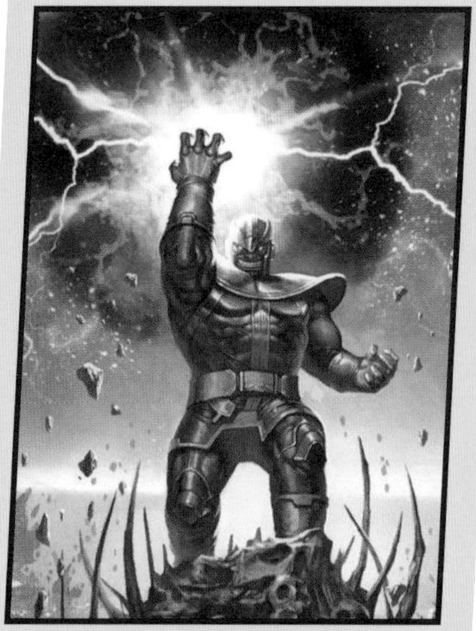

Death's companion

When Death appeared to Thanos in the form of a woman, he became obsessed with winning her love. Desperate to impress her, Thanos used a huge army to destroy many worlds across the universe.

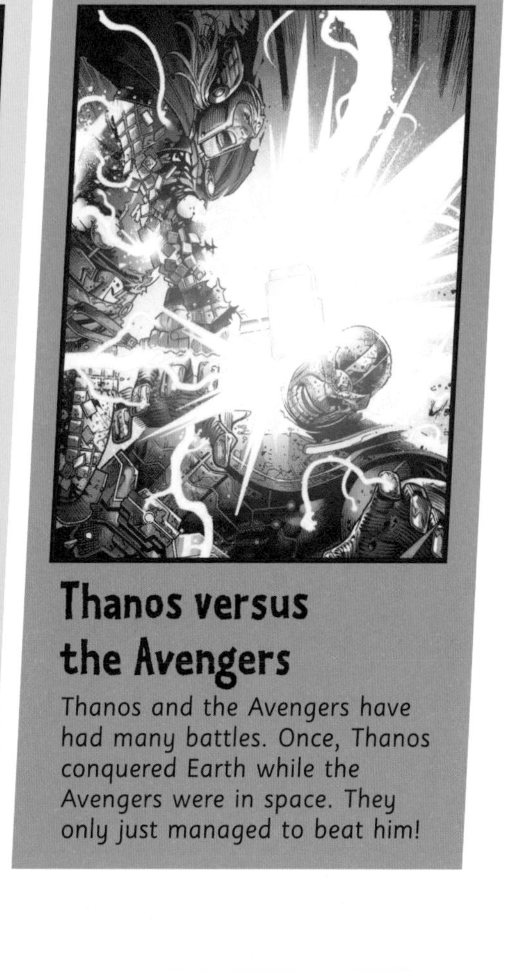

Thanos versus the Avengers

Thanos and the Avengers have had many battles. Once, Thanos conquered Earth while the Avengers were in space. They only just managed to beat him!

Infinity Gauntlet

Thanos created the Infinity Gauntlet to hold six Infinity Gems. Each gem has a different power, and when Thanos used all six to complete the Gauntlet, he became incredibly powerful.

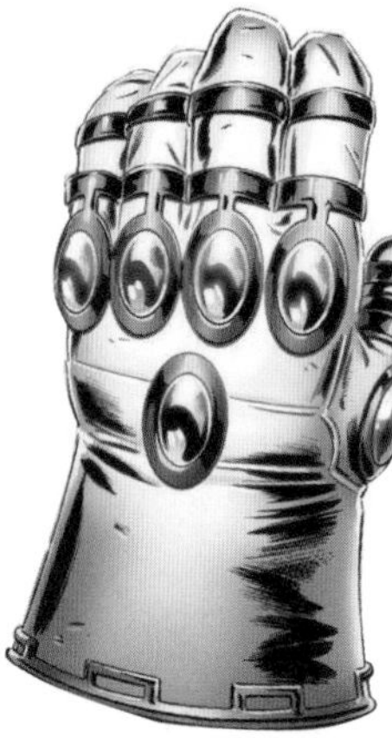

Vast strength

Thanos has almost limitless strength. He has destroyed entire planets with a single blow!

Thanos's skin is a light **purple**.

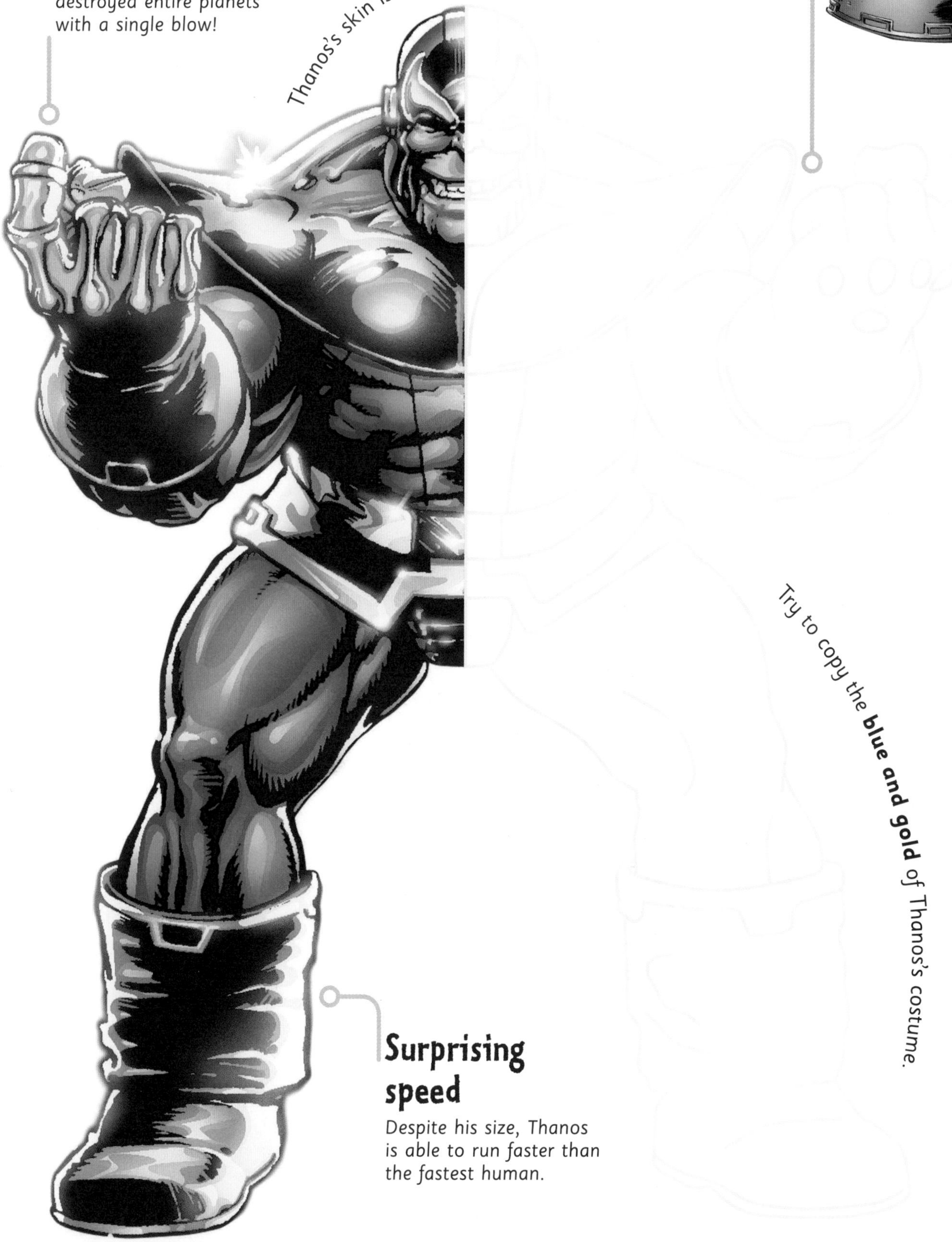

Try to copy the **blue and gold** of Thanos's costume.

Surprising speed

Despite his size, Thanos is able to run faster than the fastest human.

Upgrade Ultron

Design new upgrades for Ultron

Ultron is an intelligent but completely evil robot, who was created by Hank Pym. Ultron is always upgrading himself, so each time the Avengers battle the terrifying robot, he is harder to defeat.

*Ultron's eyes glow **red** most of the time.*

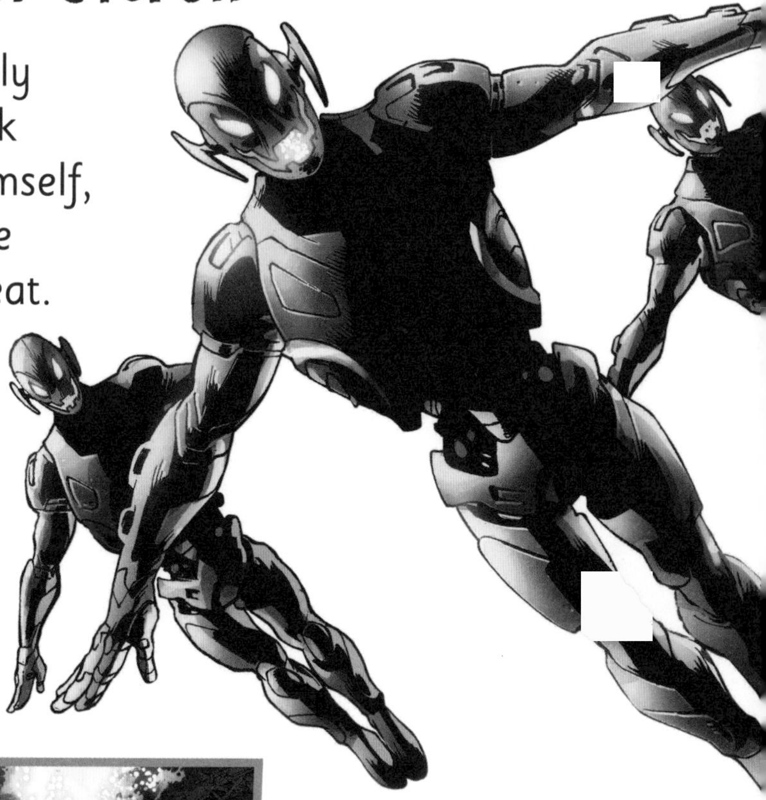

Read about Ultron and draw new upgrades for him, then write what they can do.

Army of Ultrons

Ultron created many copies of himself in order to take over Earth. They even had special built-in sensors to track down Super Heroes.

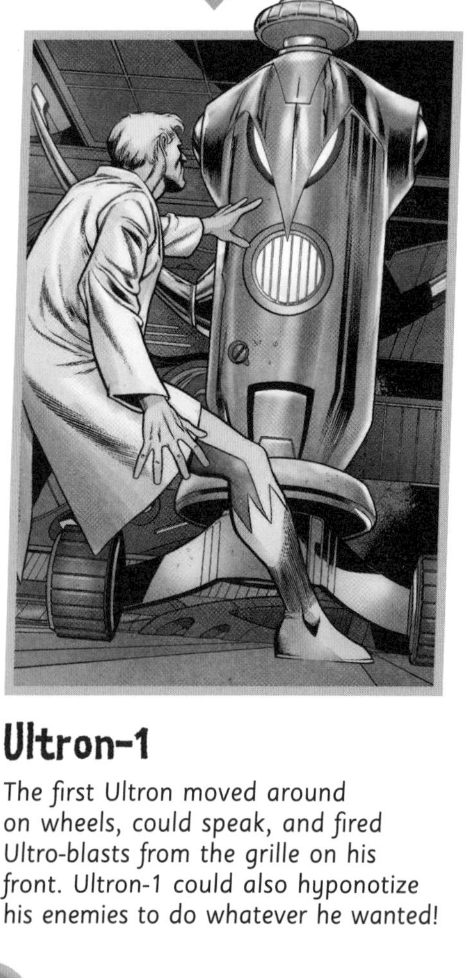

Ultron-1

The first Ultron moved around on wheels, could speak, and fired Ultro-blasts from the grille on his front. Ultron-1 could also hyponotize his enemies to do whatever he wanted!

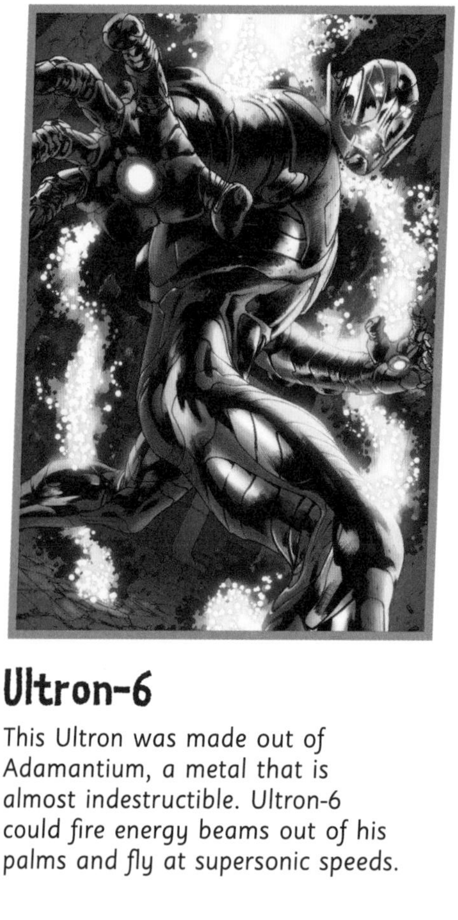

Ultron-6

This Ultron was made out of Adamantium, a metal that is almost indestructible. Ultron-6 could fire energy beams out of his palms and fly at supersonic speeds.

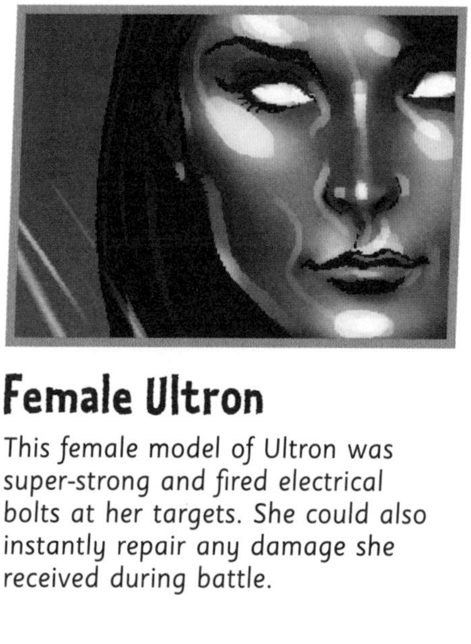

Female Ultron

This female model of Ultron was super-strong and fired electrical bolts at her targets. She could also instantly repair any damage she received during battle.

Draw a new type of **body** for Ultron in this box.

Draw a new **head** for Ultron in this box.

My Ultron head upgrade can:

✏ _____

_____

You could draw Ultron as a **vehicle**.

Draw a new **arm** with **a gadget** in this box.

You could draw Ultron with **claws**.

My Ultron arm upgrade can:

✏ _____

_____

My Ultron body upgrade can:

✏ _____

_____

Masters of Evil!

Create a recruitment poster

The Masters of Evil are a team of sinister Super Villains. The group was created by the dastardly Baron Zemo. There have been many members over the years, but the original team included Melter, Black Knight, and Radioactive Man.

Read about the Masters of Evil, then find the stickers of them and complete the poster.

Black Knight

Black Knight was once a gifted scientist. After turning to crime, he created a winged horse for himself called Elendil. Black Knight wears a black suit of armor and carries a special power lance.

Baron Zemo

Zemo was once a top scientist who liked testing his evil creations on innocent people. When Captain America fought him, a special glue he had invented splashed on his face, sticking his purple hood to his skin forever.

Melter

Melter is a failed businessman with a grudge against Iron Man. He uses a special melting ray mounted on his chest, which can melt iron almost instantly.

Radioactive Man

Dr. Chen Lu was once a respected nuclear physicist. He exposed himself to radiation while trying to find a way to defeat Thor. Now, he can shoot blasts of radiation out of his body.

Add stickers of **Melter**, **Black Knight**, and **Radioactive Man**.

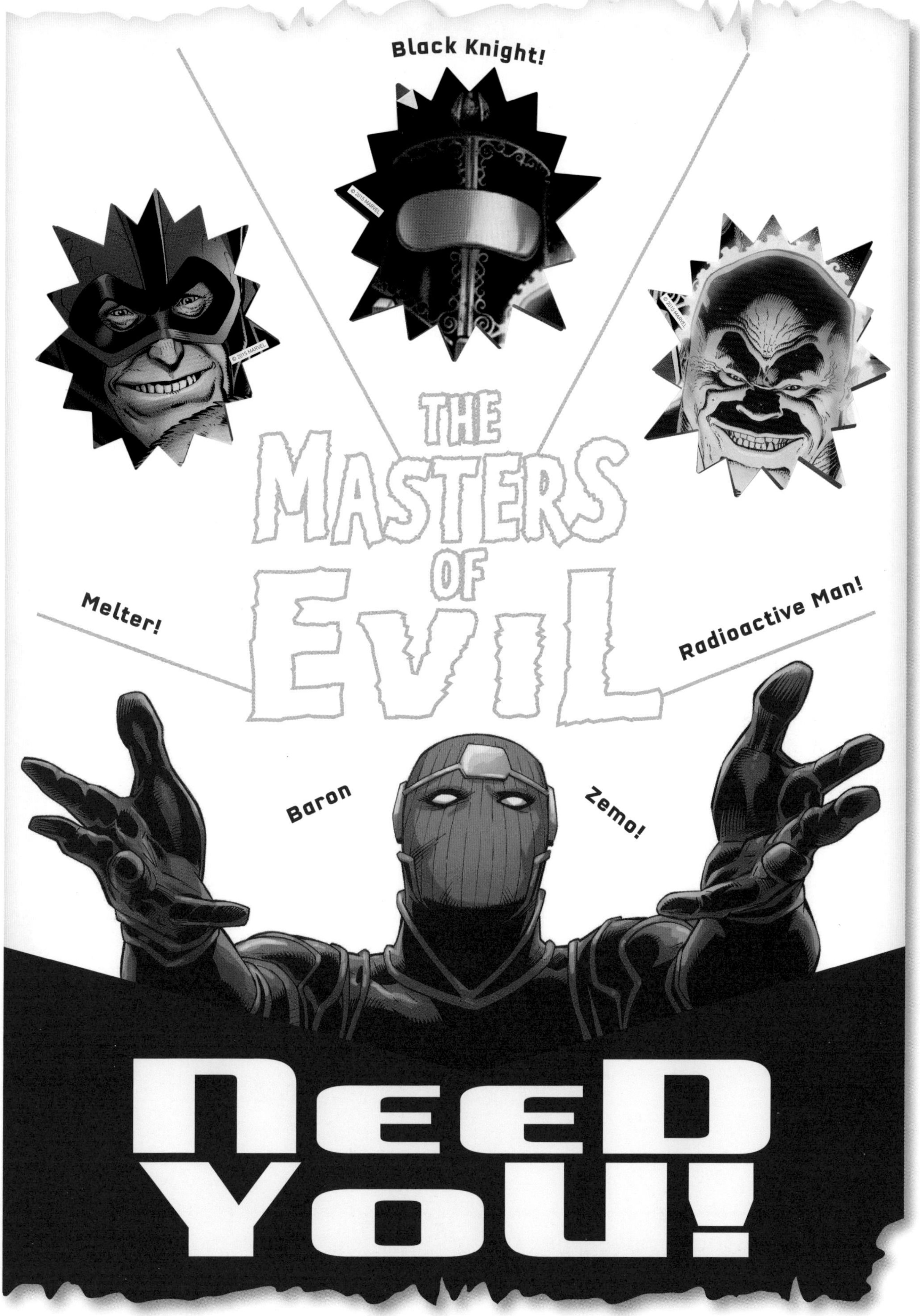
Black Knight!
THE MASTERS OF EVIL
Melter!
Radioactive Man!
Baron
Zemo!
NEED YOU!

Fill in the backgrounds behind the villains. You could simply **color them in**, or **draw a scene**!

Color in the **writing** on the poster.

Find the **stickers** at the back of the book.

Chapter 3 Challenge

Test your knowledge of this chapter

Answer each question. If you need help, look back through the section.

Now you have finished the third chapter of the book, take the Challenge to show what you have learned!

1. Find the sticker that best matches the description:

This wicked villain wears purple and suffered a sticky situation with his hood.

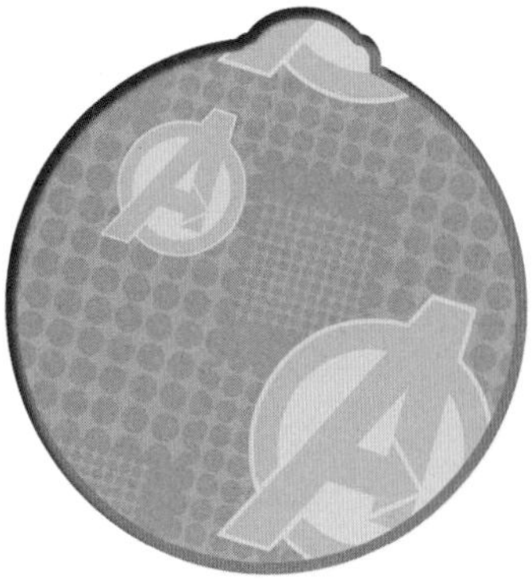

2. Who was the Avengers' very first enemy?

Egghead ☐ **Loki** ☐ **Ultron** ☐

3. Attuma's powers grow weaker as he gets closer to water.

True ☐ **False** ☐

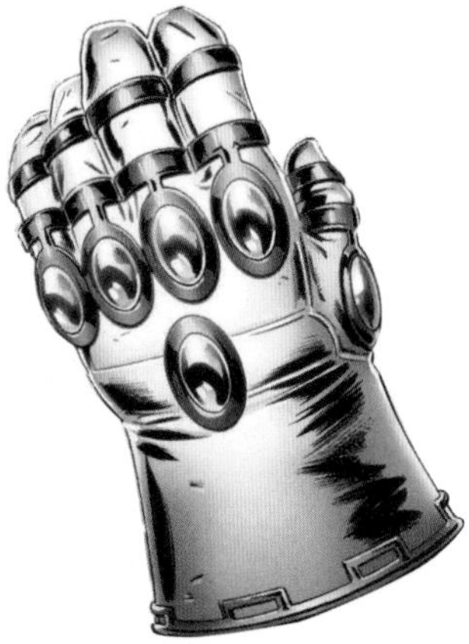

4. What is the name of this mighty jeweled object?

✎ ______________________________

5. ✎ ______________________________ has photographic reflexes, that enable him to copy his foes' fighting moves.

Find the **answers** on page 97.

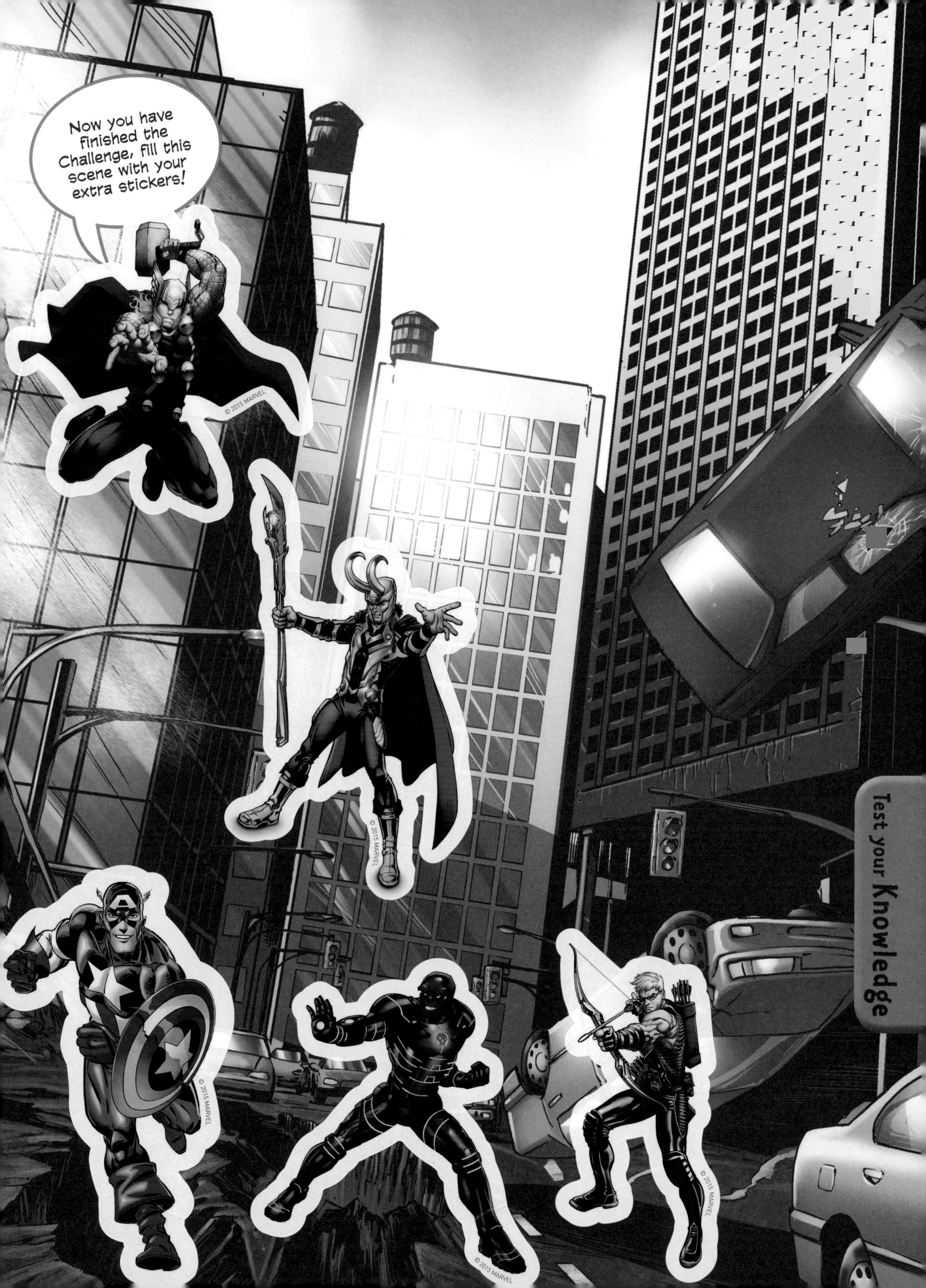
Now you have finished the Challenge, fill this scene with your extra stickers!
© 2015 MARVEL
© 2015 MARVEL
© 2015 MARVEL
© 2015 MARVEL
© 2015 MARVEL

CHAPTER 4 Epic battles

The Skrulls

The Skrulls are an alien race who have tried to invade Earth. They have many powers including the ability to change their appearance. No one is safe—not even the Avengers!

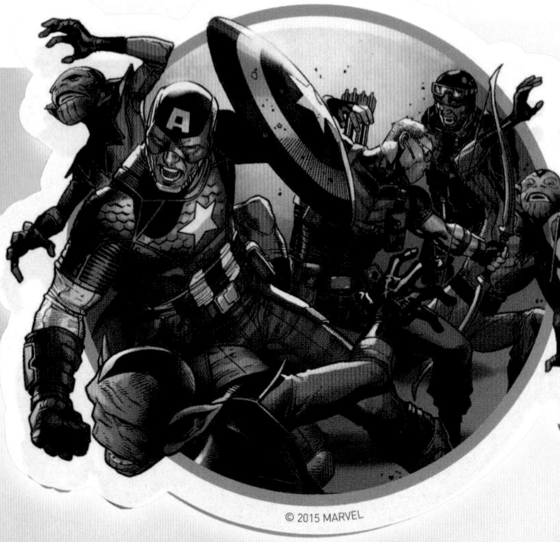

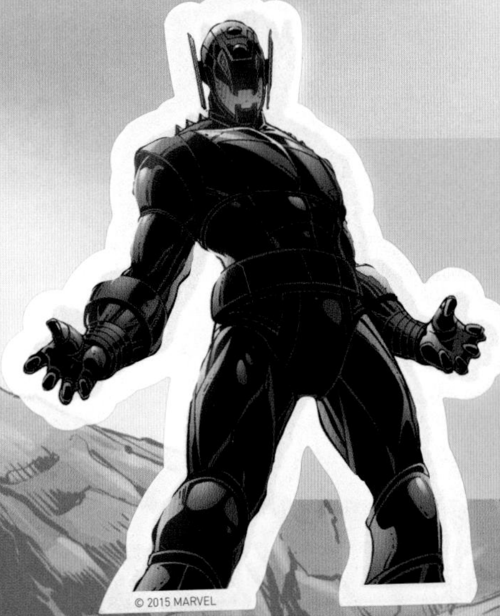

Ultron attacks!

Every time the Avengers think that they have finally beaten this evil robot, he comes back, even more powerful than before. Ultron will not stop until he has destroyed all life!

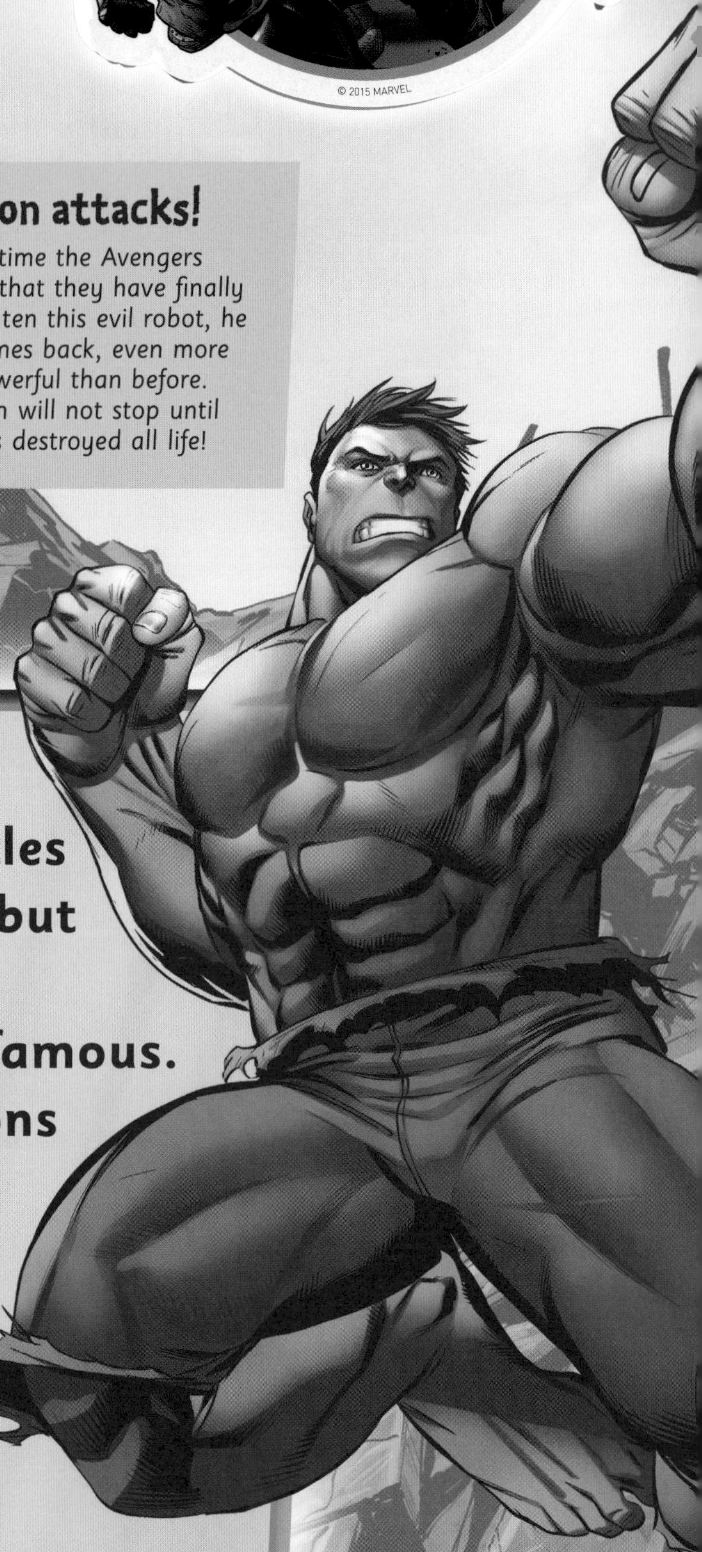

The Avengers have fought countless battles to protect the Earth, but some conflicts have become particularly famous. Massive alien invasions have threatened the entire planet, and some Avengers have even fought epic personal grudge matches.

Find the **stickers** at the back of the book.

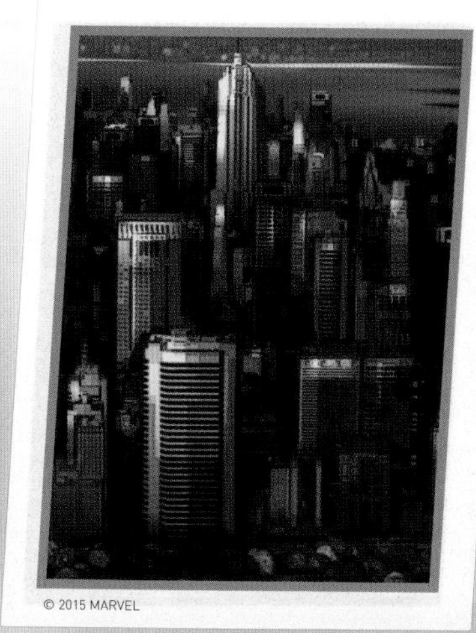
© 2015 MARVEL

New York City

The Avengers live in New York City. It is one of the greatest cities in the world, so it is often a target for Super Villains and alien invasions. This means the Avengers are usually near the scene of the action.

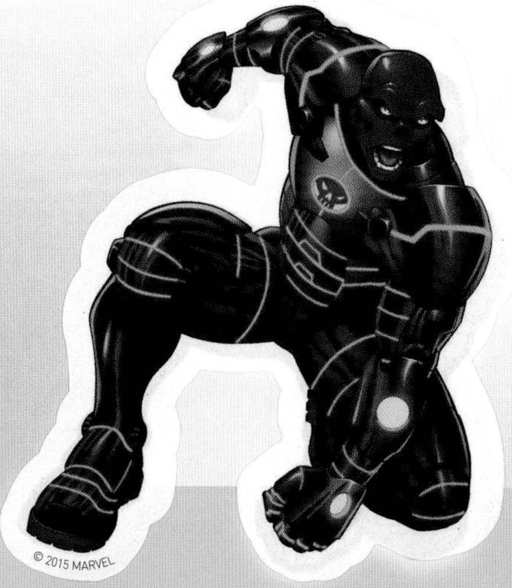
© 2015 MARVEL

The Red Skull

Captain America's oldest enemy is the evil Red Skull, who was once a scientist named Johann Schmidt. They fought each other during World War II, and now the Red Skull is determined to destroy Cap.

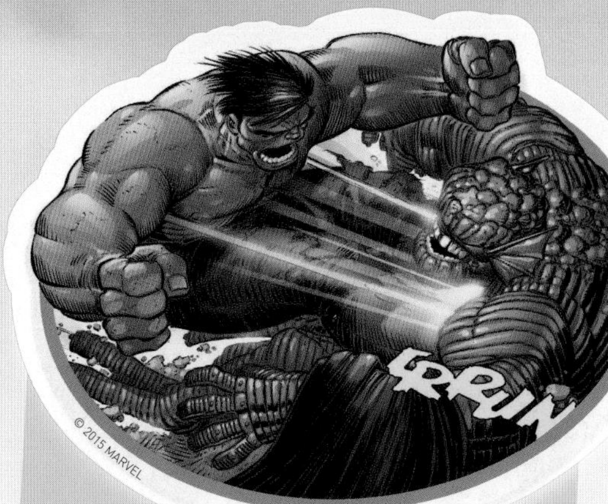
© 2015 MARVEL

Hulk and Abomination

After being hit by gamma radiation in the lab of Dr. Bruce Banner (AKA the Hulk), Russian spy Emil Blonsky turned into a monster. He became known as Abomination, and swore vengeance on the Hulk.

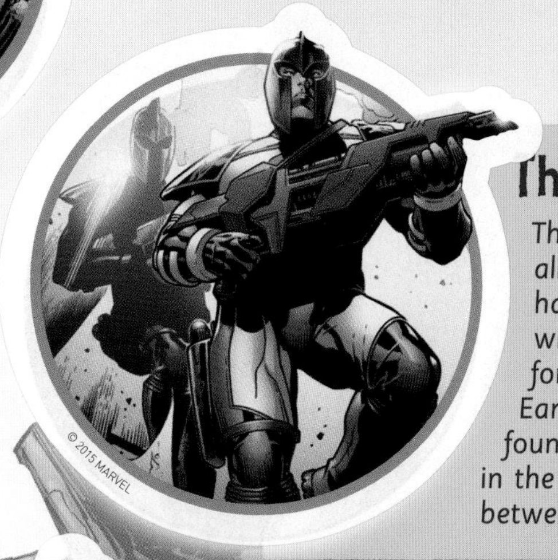
© 2015 MARVEL

The Kree

The Kree are another alien species. They have been at war with the Skrulls for a million years. Earth has often found itself caught in the middle of battles between the two races.

Fact Challenge

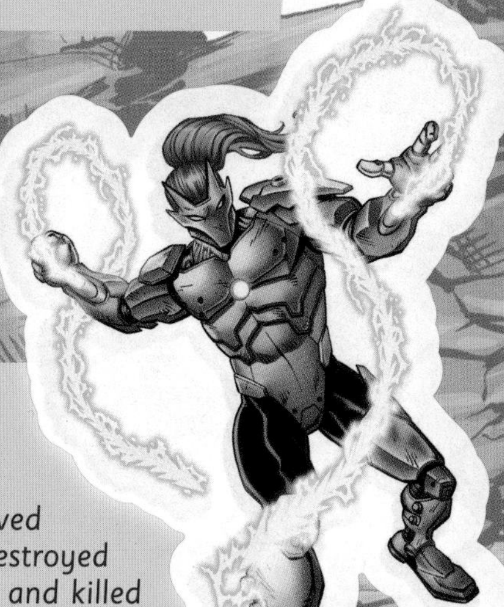
© 2015 MARVEL

Whiplash

Anton Vanko mistakenly believed that Iron Man destroyed his home village and killed his father. He created his own power suit with two built-in energy whips, and set out for revenge.

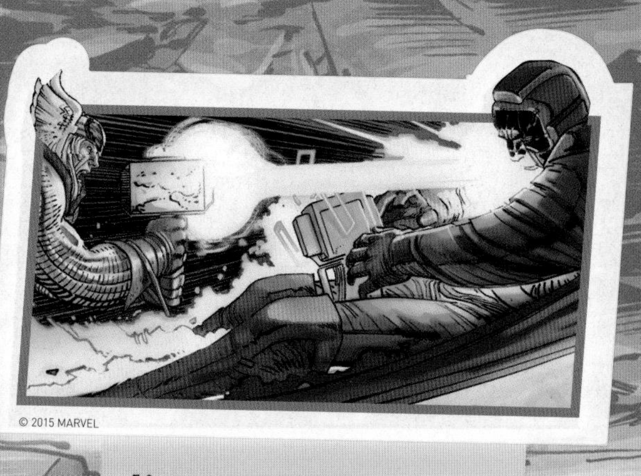
© 2015 MARVEL

Kang

Kang's advanced weaponry makes him a lethal enemy. To defeat him, the Avengers must first outsmart him.

Secret Invasion

Write your own newspaper story

The Skrulls are an alien species from Skrullos, who have the amazing ability to change their appearance to look like anyone they want. They enjoy conquering other planets.

The Skrulls used many powerful spaceships to travel to Earth.

Read about the Secret Invasion and then write a newspaper article about it.

1 Alien invaders

- **The Skrulls** want to take over **Earth** because they believe that the Avengers are a **threat** to them.
- While they prepare their terrifying army, they secretly send **Skrull agents** to Earth.

2 Imposters

- The Skrull agents **kidnap Hank Pym** and other important heroes.
- The Skrulls **impersonate** them and damage Earth's defenses.

3 Skrulls revealed

- The Avengers realize that Hank Pym is an imposter, but **the Skrull army attacks** before the Avengers can prepare for it.
- After a fierce battle, the Avengers **successfully defeat** the Skrulls.

4 Friends reunited

- The Skrulls **escape** in their **spaceships**, but leave one behind in Central Park.
- On board, the heroes find all of their kidnapped **friends** alive and well.

Decide what the most **important** parts of the story are.

Remember to draw a **picture** to go with your story.

DAILY BUGLE

New York City

ALIEN ATTACK
DEVASTATES THE PLANET

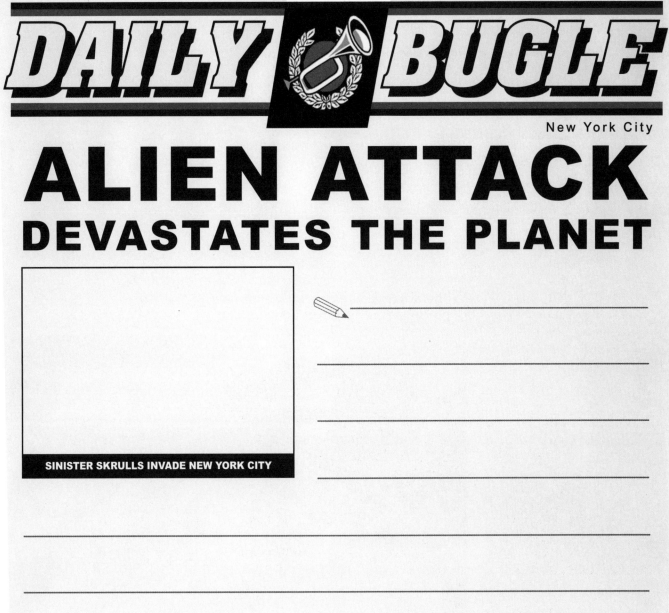

SINISTER SKRULLS INVADE NEW YORK CITY

Think about the most **exciting way** to describe the Secret Invasion.

Conquer Kang!

Finish the comic strip

Kang the Conqueror is a time-traveling villain from the 30th century. In the future, he has a big empire and loves to fight anyone that gets in his way.

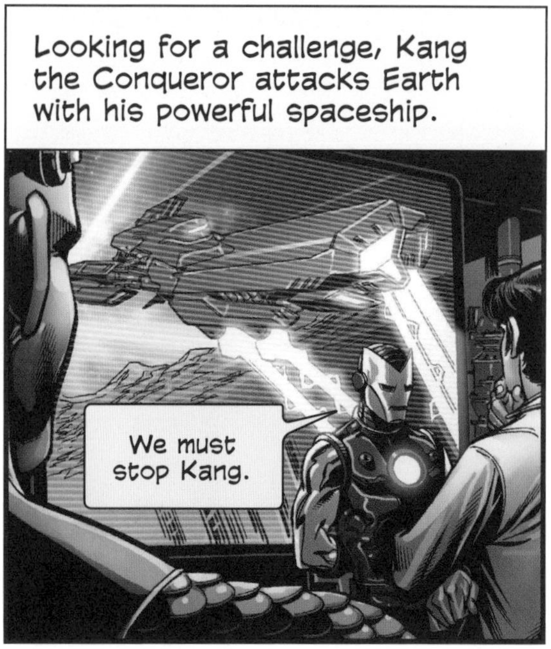
Looking for a challenge, Kang the Conqueror attacks Earth with his powerful spaceship.
We must stop Kang.

Read the story and then write and draw the ending. Use these pictures to help you with your drawing.

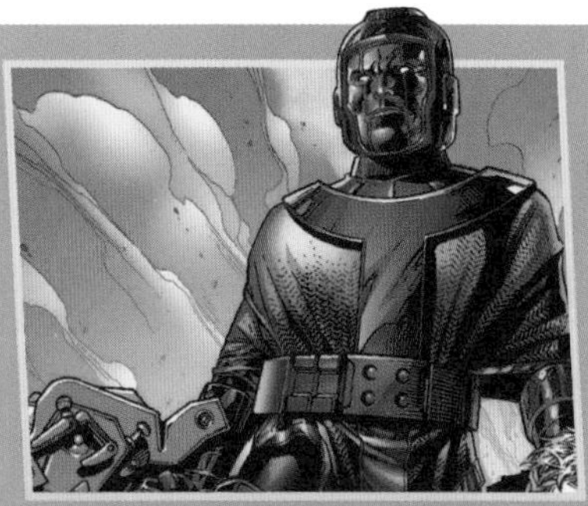

Kang's armor

Kang's green and purple suit makes him super-strong. It also has a built-in energy shield and lets him hover in the air.

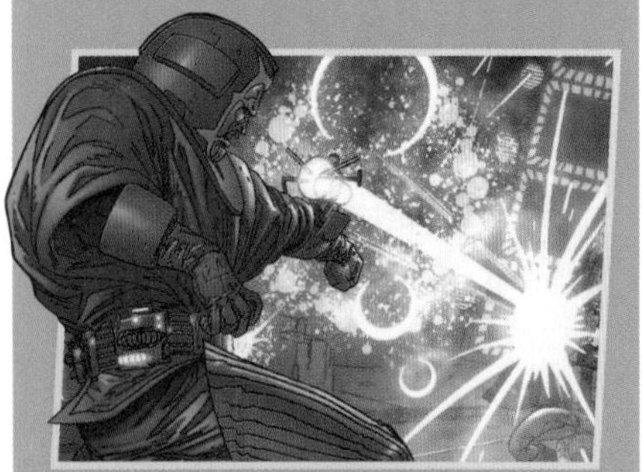

Futuristic weapons

Kang uses weapons from the future to defeat his enemies. His favorites include hand-sized missile launchers and wrist-mounted lasers.

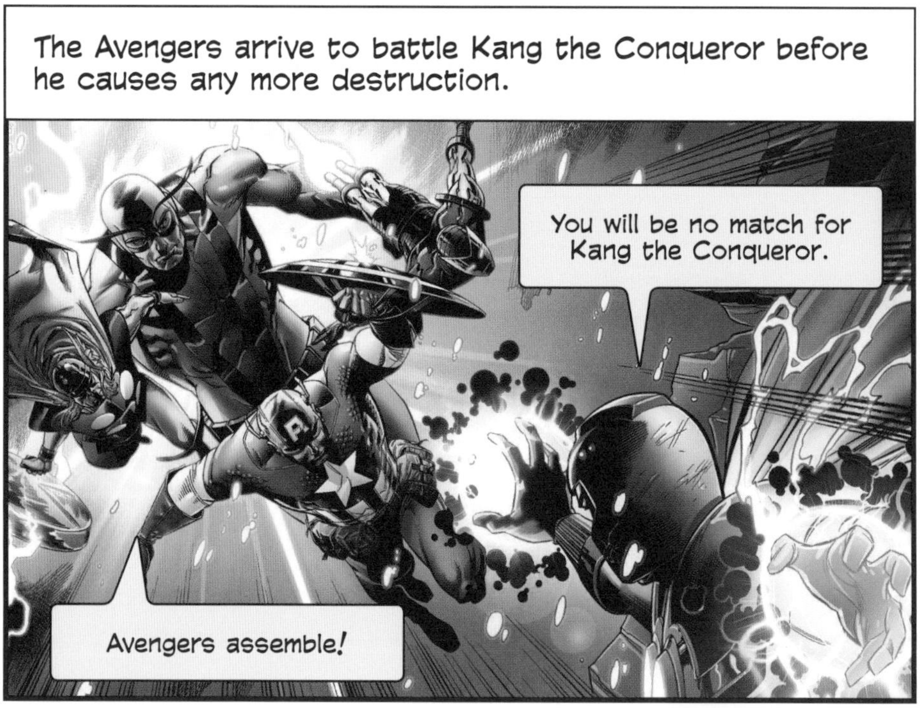
The Avengers arrive to battle Kang the Conqueror before he causes any more destruction.
You will be no match for Kang the Conqueror.
Avengers assemble!

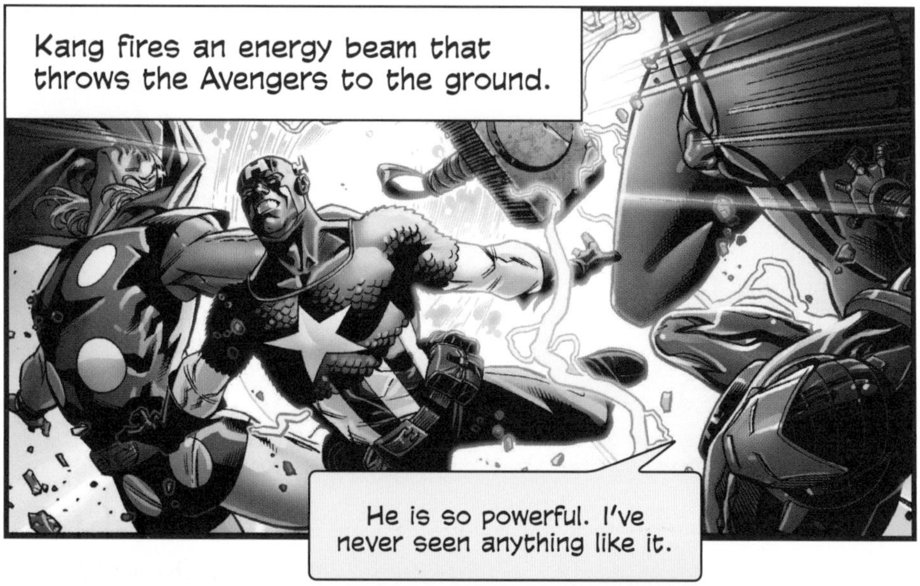
Kang fires an energy beam that throws the Avengers to the ground.
He is so powerful. I've never seen anything like it.

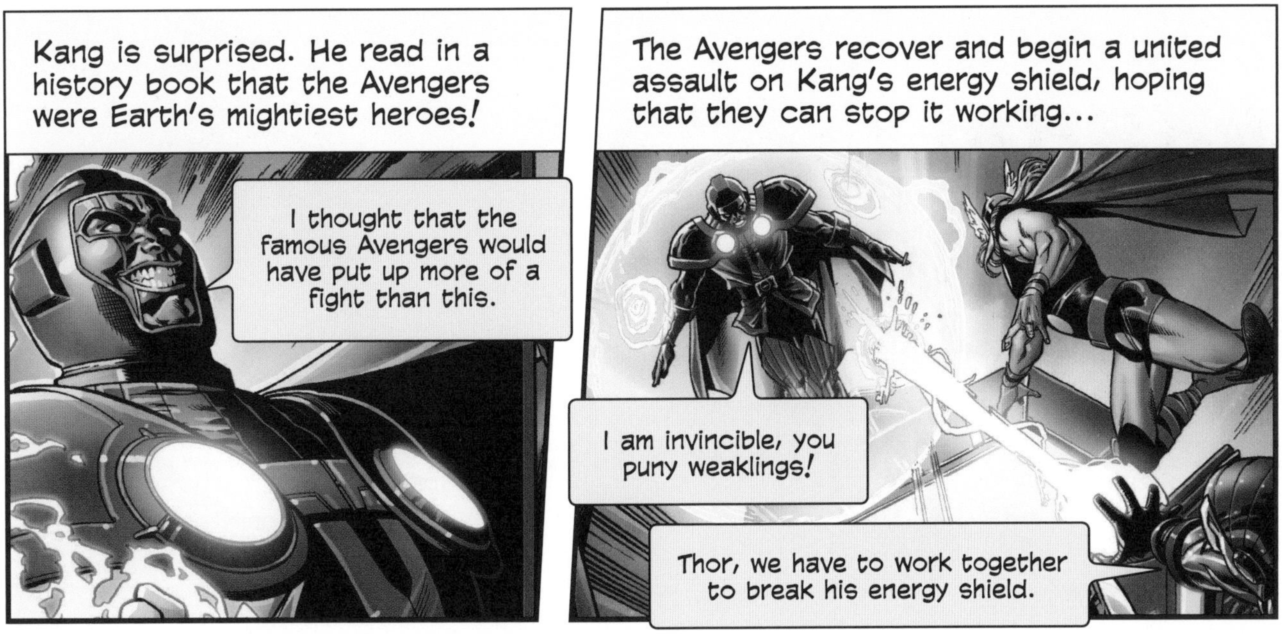
Kang is surprised. He read in a history book that the Avengers were Earth's mightiest heroes!
I thought that the famous Avengers would have put up more of a fight than this.
The Avengers recover and begin a united assault on Kang's energy shield, hoping that they can stop it working...
I am invincible, you puny weaklings!
Thor, we have to work together to break his energy shield.

Start drawing **lightly** with a **pencil** before you use colored pens or pencils.

How will the story **end**? You **decide**!

THE END!

You could include **speech bubbles** for the characters.

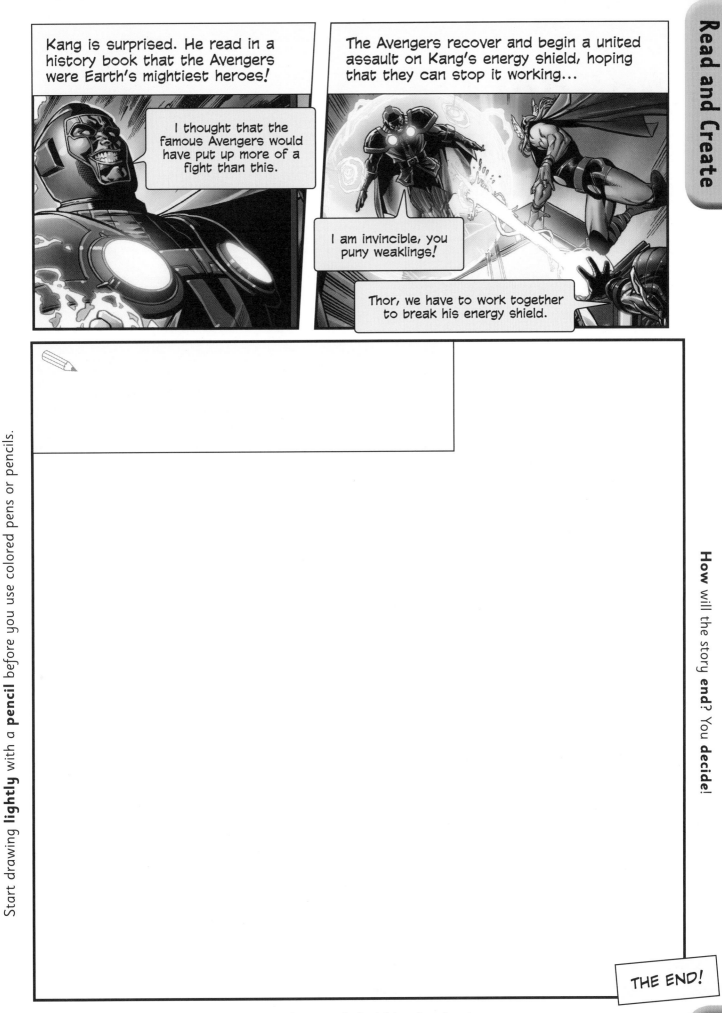

Avengers Assemble!

Help the Avengers cross the city

When the Avengers have to meet up at Stark Tower, the ones who can't fly have to travel through the streets of New York City. This can be really dangerous. No one knows who or what they might run into along the way!

Read the instructions to begin the mission.

The mission

1. Grab something to use as a counter, and place it at the start.

2. Ask a friend to join you on your mission. Decide who wants to be Captain America, Black Widow, or Hawkeye:

Captain America's tactical knowledge means he is ready to deal with any emergency.

Hawkeye's bow and trick arrows allow him to deal with any situation.

Black Widow's spy training and high-tech gear can get her out of any tight spot.

3. Decide who will go first. Take turns to roll a die, then move the number of spaces that are shown on the die.

4. Be the first person to reach Stark Tower.

5. Watch out for hazards along the way!

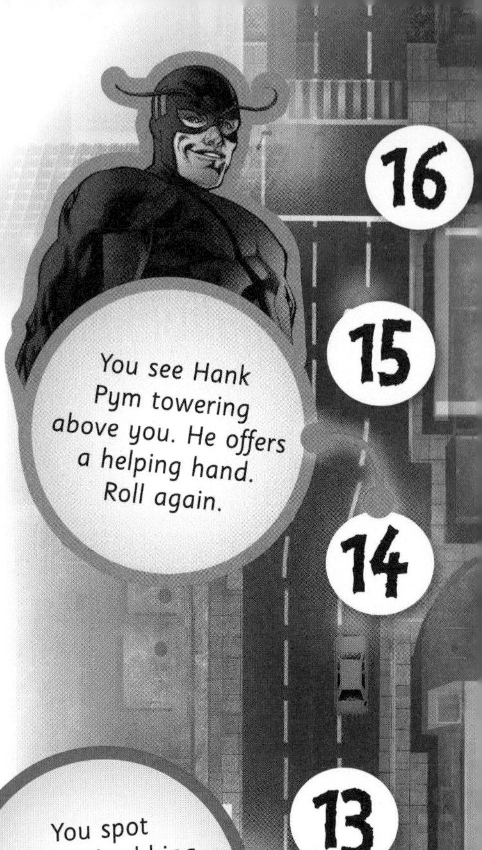
16
15
You see Hank Pym towering above you. He offers a helping hand. Roll again.
14

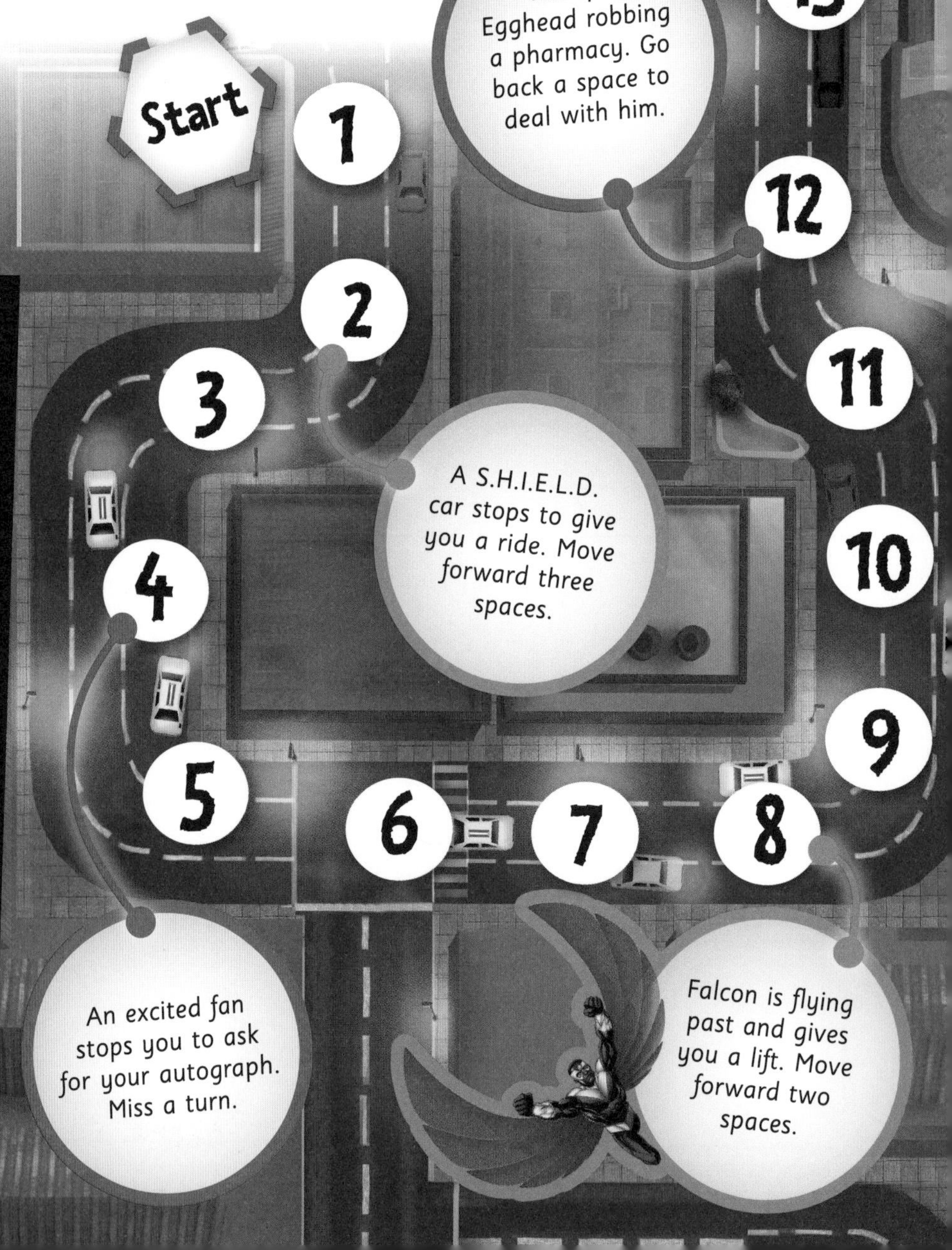
Start
1
2
3
4
5
6
7
8
9
10
11
12
13
You spot Egghead robbing a pharmacy. Go back a space to deal with him.
A S.H.I.E.L.D. car stops to give you a ride. Move forward three spaces.
An excited fan stops you to ask for your autograph. Miss a turn.
Falcon is flying past and gives you a lift. Move forward two spaces.

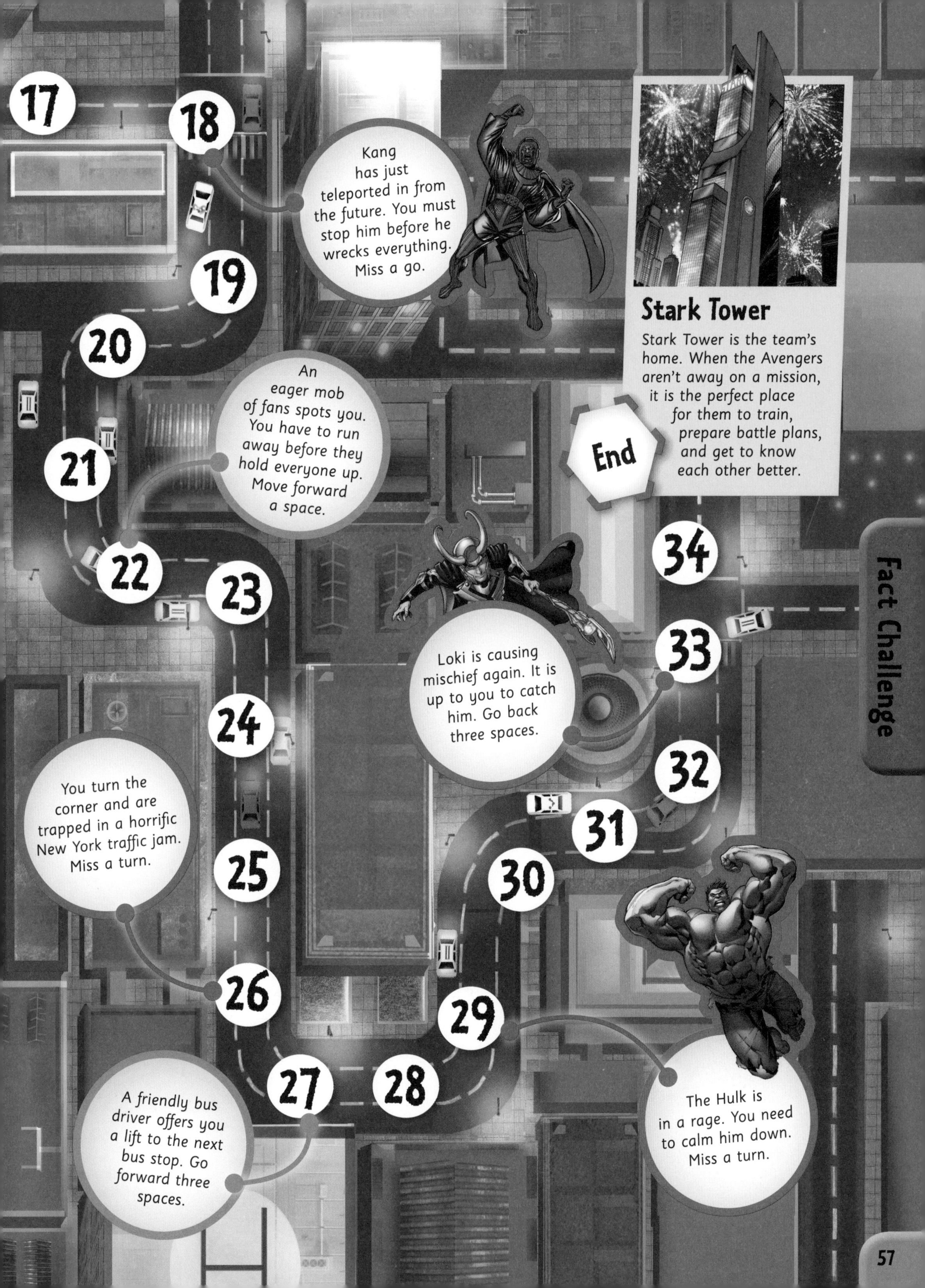
17
18
Kang has just teleported in from the future. You must stop him before he wrecks everything. Miss a go.
19
20
An eager mob of fans spots you. You have to run away before they hold everyone up. Move forward a space.
21
22
23
24
You turn the corner and are trapped in a horrific New York traffic jam. Miss a turn.
25
26
27
A friendly bus driver offers you a lift to the next bus stop. Go forward three spaces.
28
29
The Hulk is in a rage. You need to calm him down. Miss a turn.
30
31
32
33
Loki is causing mischief again. It is up to you to catch him. Go back three spaces.
34
End

Stark Tower

Stark Tower is the team's home. When the Avengers aren't away on a mission, it is the perfect place for them to train, prepare battle plans, and get to know each other better.

Revenge of Ultron

Color in the Avengers

Ultron and the Avengers have had many battles over the years. The Avengers have to work as a team, using their different fighting styles to take him down.

Read about the Avengers and Ultron, then color in the scene below.

Captain America's costume is **red**, **white**, and **blue**.

Fighting styles

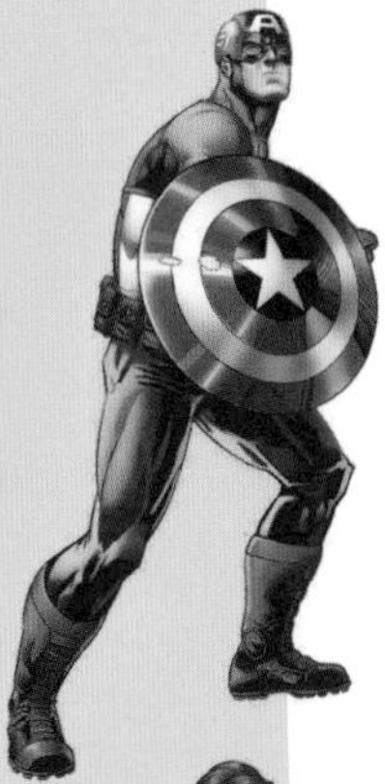

Captain America

Captain America uses his Vibranium shield to absorb Ultron's energy blasts. He also uses it as a weapon to attack this villain.

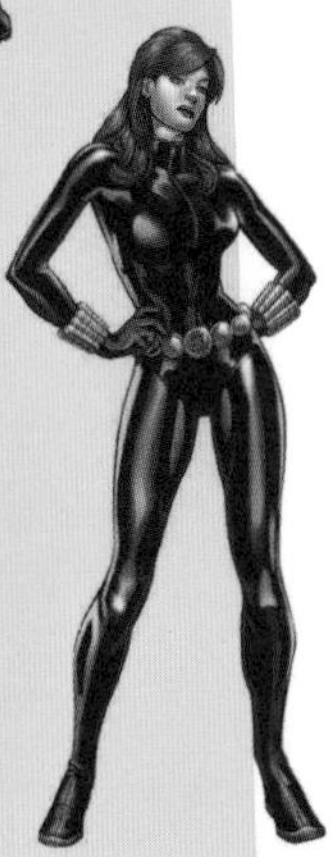

Black Widow

Black Widow can easily dodge Ultron's powerful attacks. She can use her Widow's Bite to stun this evil robot.

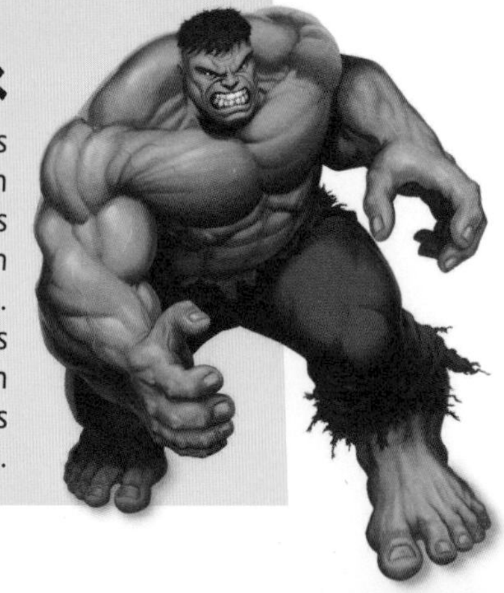

The Hulk

The Hulk's incredibly tough skin stops Ultron from harming him. Hulk uses his super-strength to defeat this robotic foe.

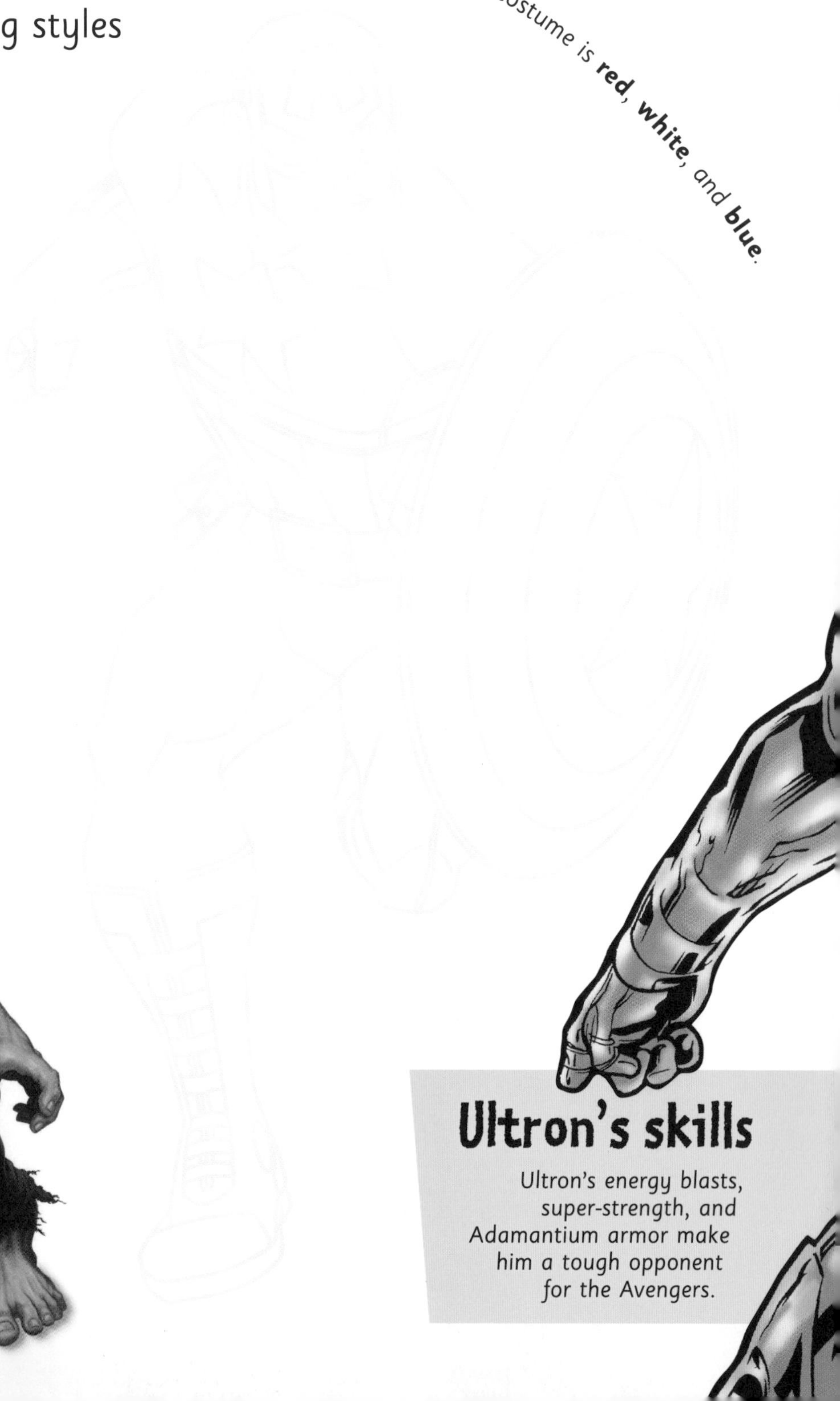

Ultron's skills

Ultron's energy blasts, super-strength, and Adamantium armor make him a tough opponent for the Avengers.

Hulk's skin is **green** and his shorts are normally **purple**.

Black Widow's gauntlets and belt are **gold**.

Grudge Match!

Complete the battles

Work out which Super Villain is the archenemy of each Avenger, then find the sticker to complete the battle.

Some Super Villains and Super Heroes have long-established feuds. Caused by bitter disagreements, these grudges have led to many epic confrontations.

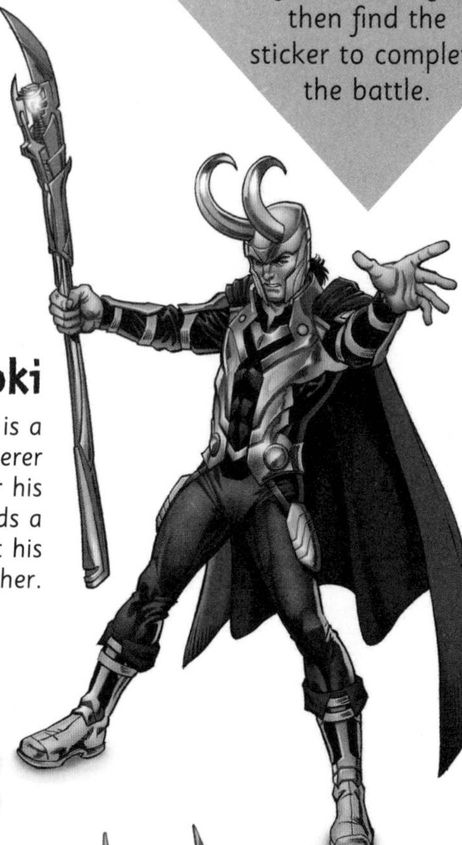

Loki

This trickster is a powerful sorcerer who can alter his shape. He holds a grudge against his adopted brother.

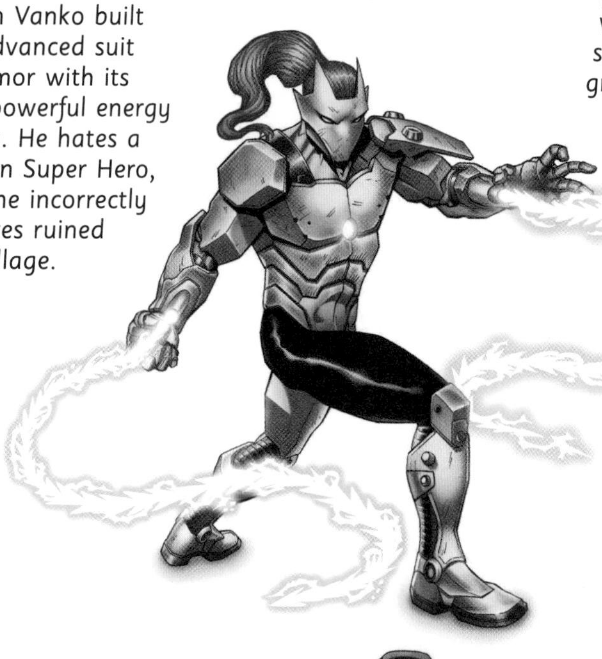

Whiplash

Anton Vanko built his advanced suit of armor with its two powerful energy whips. He hates a certain Super Hero, who he incorrectly believes ruined his village.

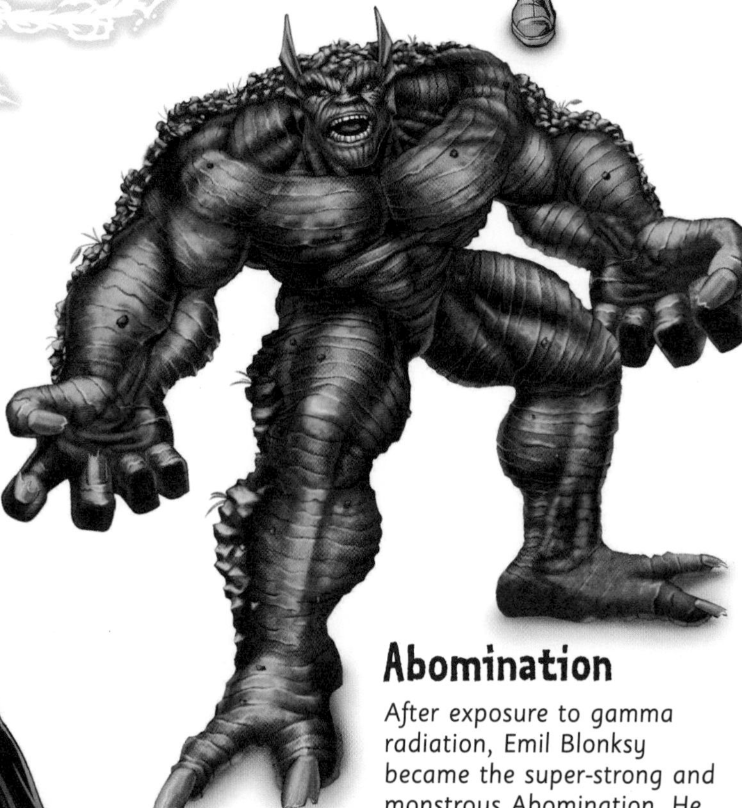

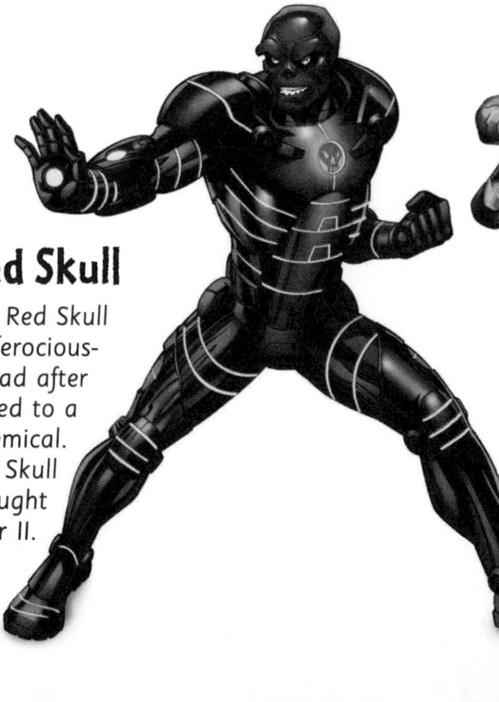

Red Skull

The villainous Red Skull gained his ferocious-looking red head after being exposed to a dangerous chemical. Both the Red Skull and his rival fought in World War II.

Abomination

After exposure to gamma radiation, Emil Blonksy became the super-strong and monstrous Abomination. He is jealous of a hero with a similar story.

Find the **stickers** at the back of the book.

Fact Challenge

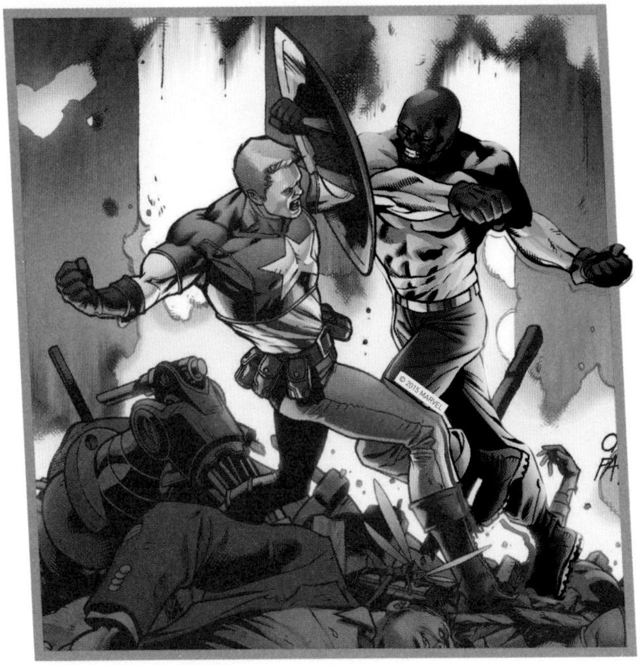
© 2015 MARVEL

1 Captain America versus

✎ ______________________

Captain America and his nemesis fought on opposite sides in **World War II**. The war has been over for many years, but the fighting between these two rivals will never end.

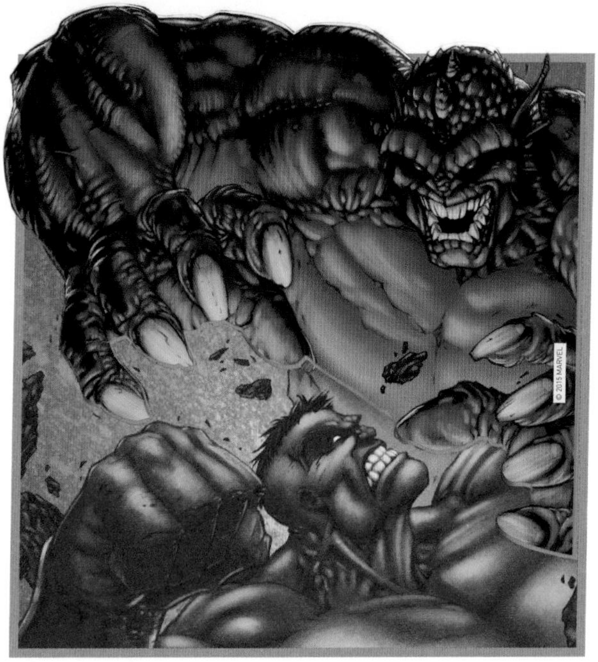
© 2015 MARVEL

2 Hulk versus

✎ ______________________

The Hulk isn't the only human who has been exposed to **gamma radiation**. His main rival also suffered the same fate and hates that the Hulk can change back to human form.

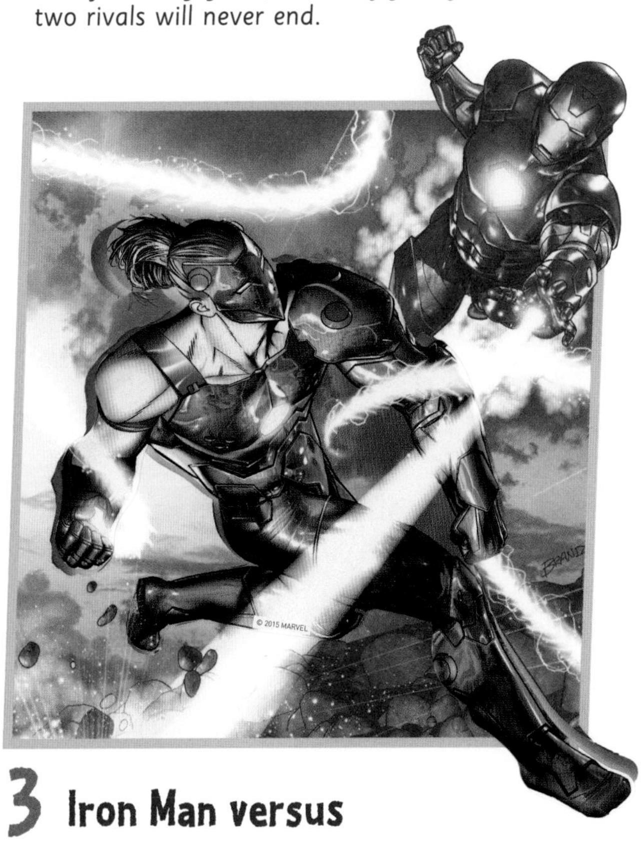
© 2015 MARVEL

3 Iron Man versus

✎ ______________________

Iron Man's rival also wears a suit of armor. This Super Villain believes that Iron Man **destroyed his village**, when it was actually an imposter.

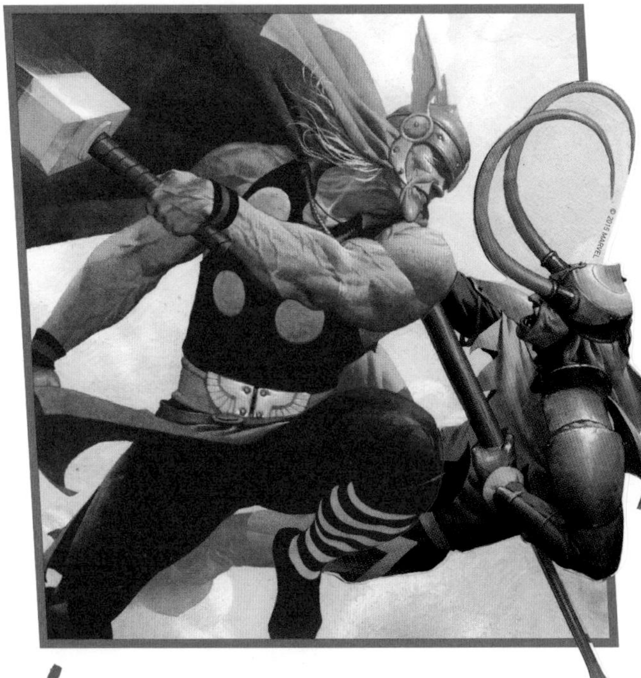
© 2015 MARVEL

4 Thor versus

✎ ______________________

This prince of Asgard made his **adopted brother** jealous because it appeared that Thor was their father's favorite child. This has caused many years of rivalry.

Find the **answers** on page 97.

Captain's Orders

Decide which Avenger to send

Read about the Avengers and their missions. Then decide who Captain America should send and find the right sticker.

Even the Avengers have bad days when there are too many emergencies for them to handle as a group. Sometimes, the Super Heroes have to split up, and it is up to Captain America to choose the right Avenger for the job.

Tactical genius

Captain America is an excellent leader because he knows his team's strengths and weaknesses. Sometimes, he remains at the Avengers' base so he can direct every mission.

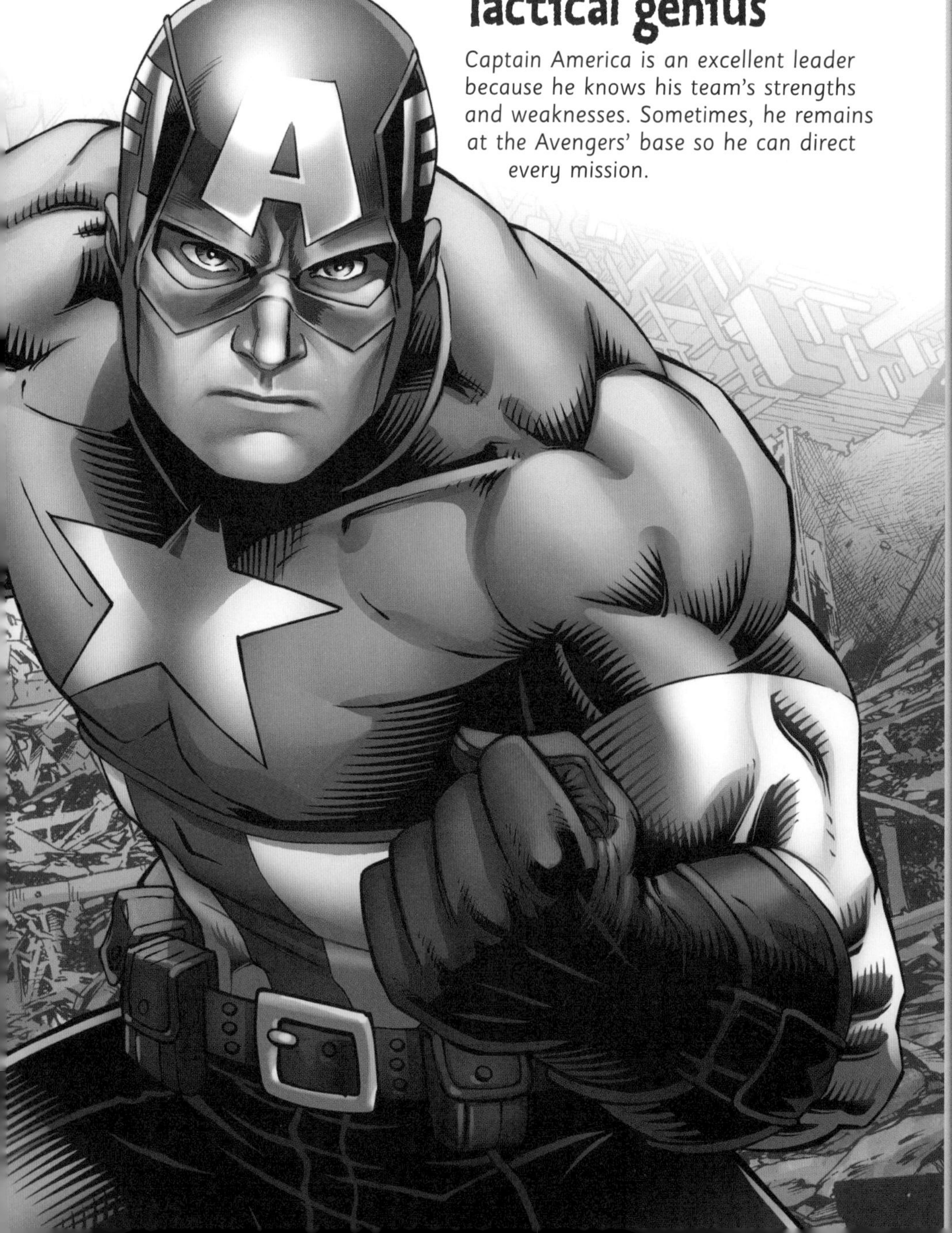

Available Avengers:

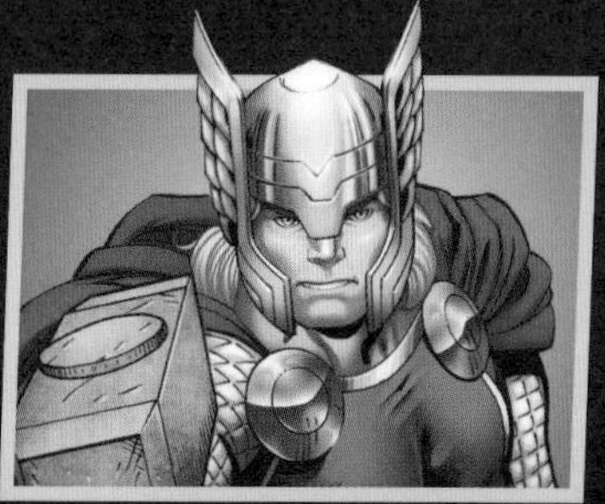

Thor

Thor is a mighty warrior who can summon lightning strikes with Mjolnir, his magical hammer.

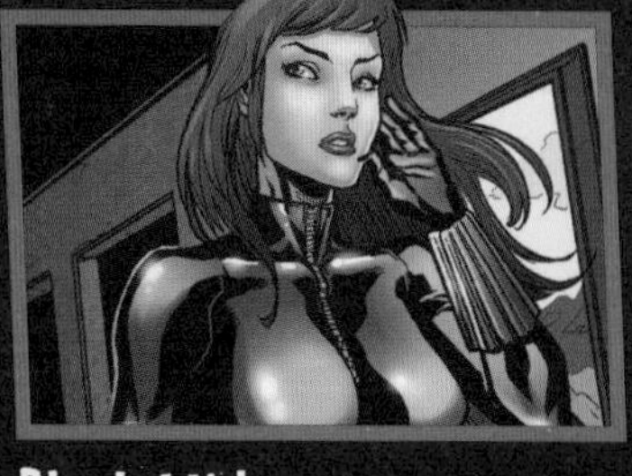

Black Widow

Before she became an Avenger, Black Widow was a spy. She uses her skills to help the Avengers.

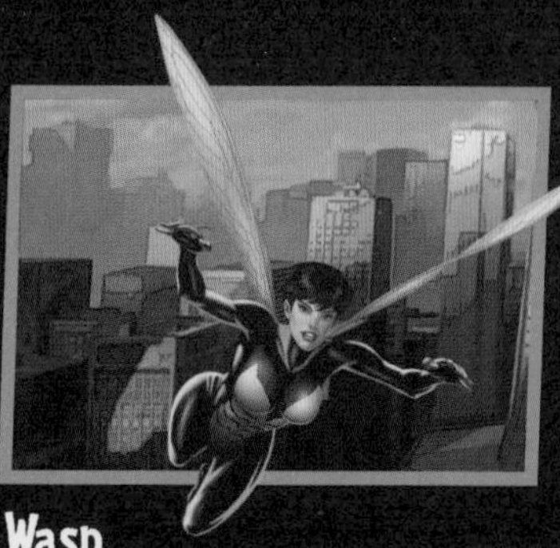

Wasp

The Wasp has the ability to shrink down to a tiny size. She can also sprout wings from her back.

You can only choose **one Avenger** for each mission, so decide **carefully**!

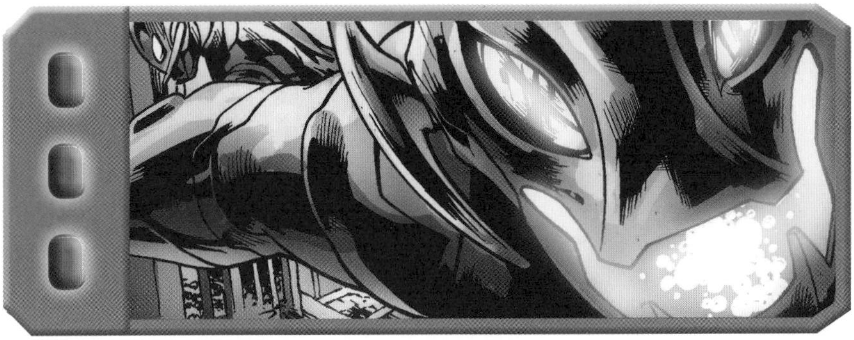

What happens next:

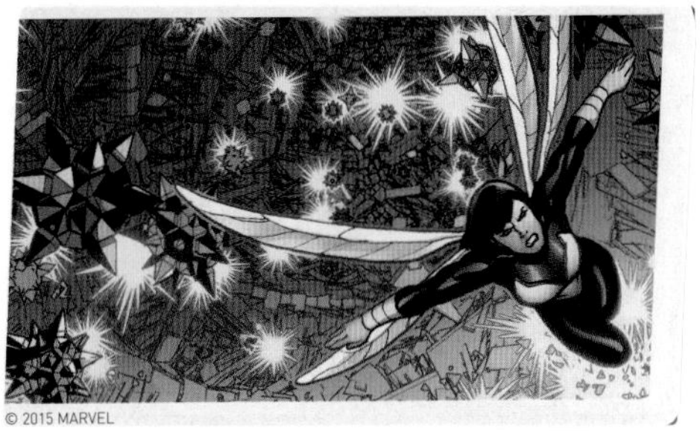
© 2015 MARVEL

1 Rampage of Ultron

Ultron is back! This time, he is attacking Times Square. Luckily, the Avengers know that Ultron can be stopped by getting inside his head and shutting him down. Captain America must send a hero who can **shrink and fly**, so they can reach Ultron's core.

Captain America will send:

Wasp

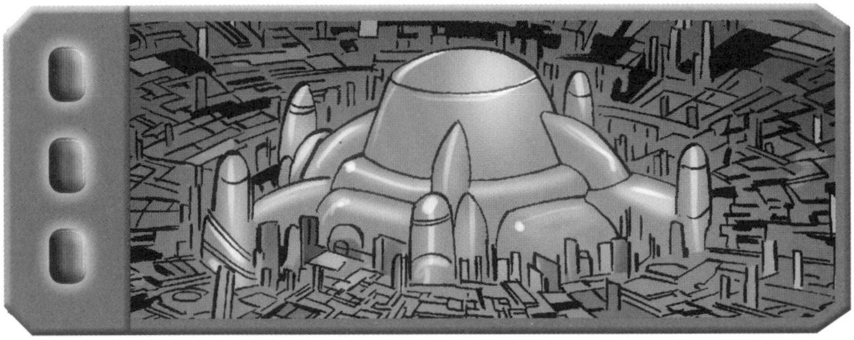

What h… next:

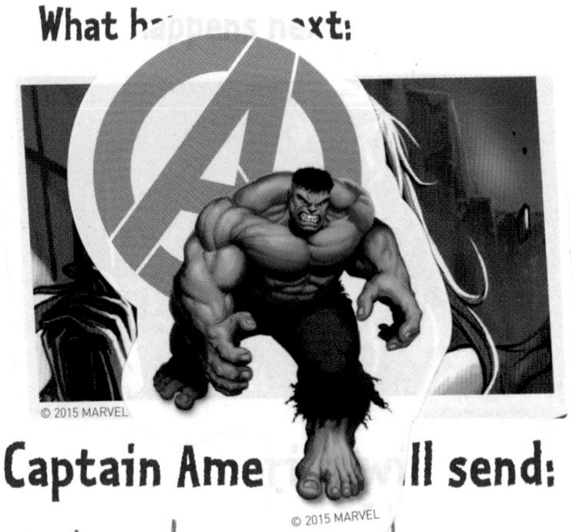
© 2015 MARVEL
© 2015 MARVEL

2 Kang's secret base

The Avengers have found a secret base in Antarctica belonging to Kang the Conqueror, where he is bound to be coming up with some evil plan. Captain America has to pick an Avenger who is superb at **spying** to find out what Kang is up to.

Captain Ame… ll send:

Black widow

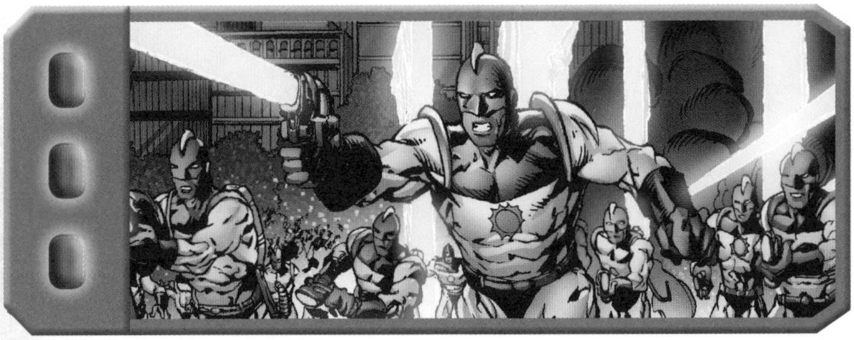

What happens next:

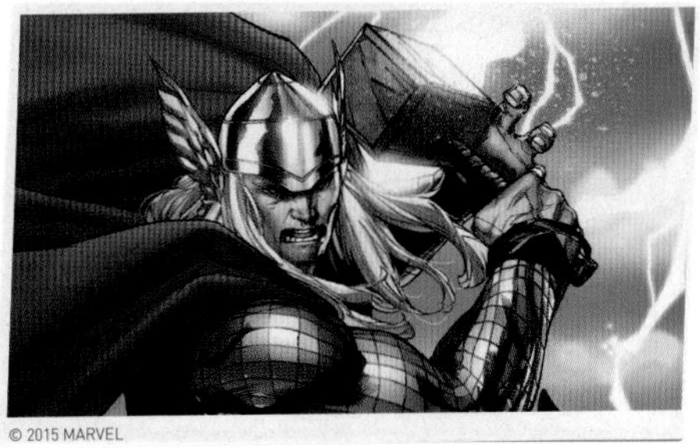
© 2015 MARVEL

3 Kree landing!

The evil, alien Kree have landed and they are planning to destroy London. Captain America needs to choose an incredibly powerful **warrior** to defeat these terrifying aliens.

Captain America will send:

Thor

Find the **stickers** at the back of the book.

Find the **answers** on page 97.

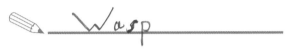

Chapter 4 Challenge

Test your knowledge of this chapter

Answer each question. If you need help, look back through the section.

Now you have finished the fourth chapter of the book, take the Challenge to see if you are a true Avengers expert!

1. Find the sticker that best matches the description:

To defeat this foe, the Avengers must be able to get to his core to shut him down.

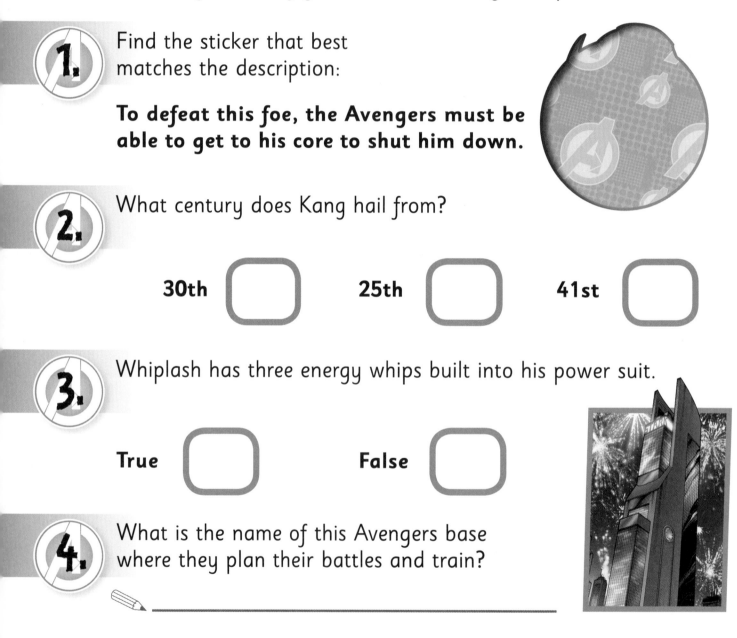

2. What century does Kang hail from?

30th ☐   25th ☐   41st ☐

3. Whiplash has three energy whips built into his power suit.

True ☐   False ☐

4. What is the name of this Avengers base where they plan their battles and train?

✎ _____

5. The evil aliens called the ✎ _____ kidnap hero Hank Pym in order to impersonate him.

Find the **answers** on page 97.

Stickers for Chapter 1

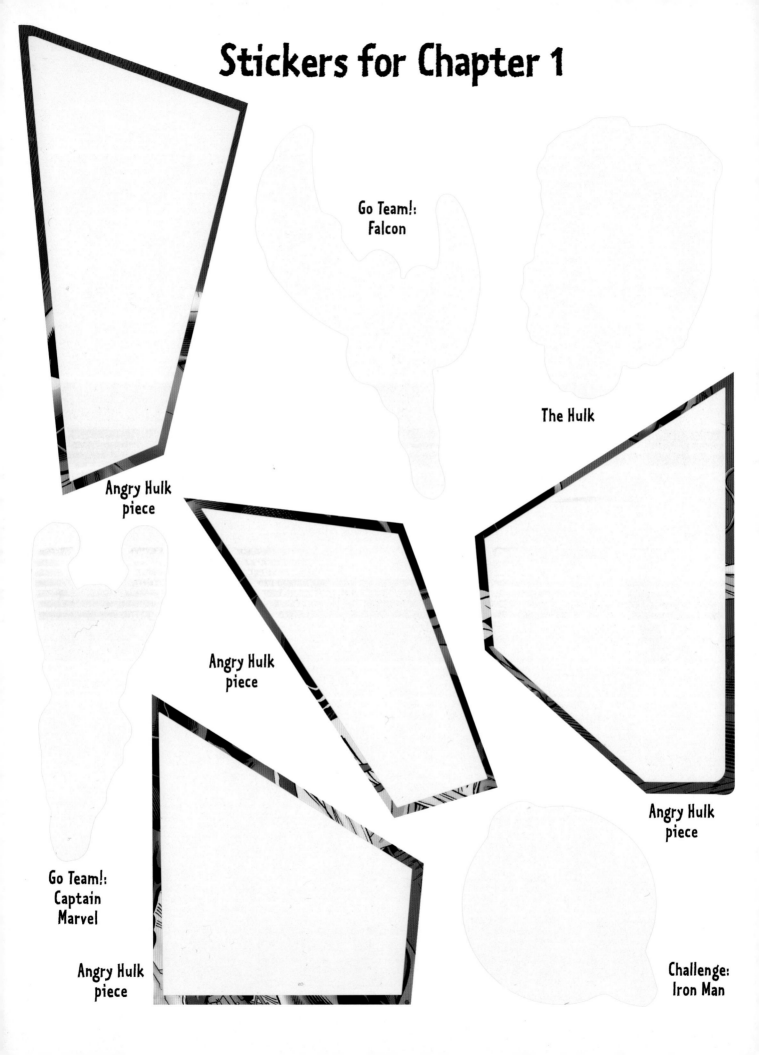

Go Team!:
Falcon

The Hulk

Angry Hulk
piece

Angry Hulk
piece

Angry Hulk
piece

Go Team!:
Captain
Marvel

Angry Hulk
piece

Challenge:
Iron Man

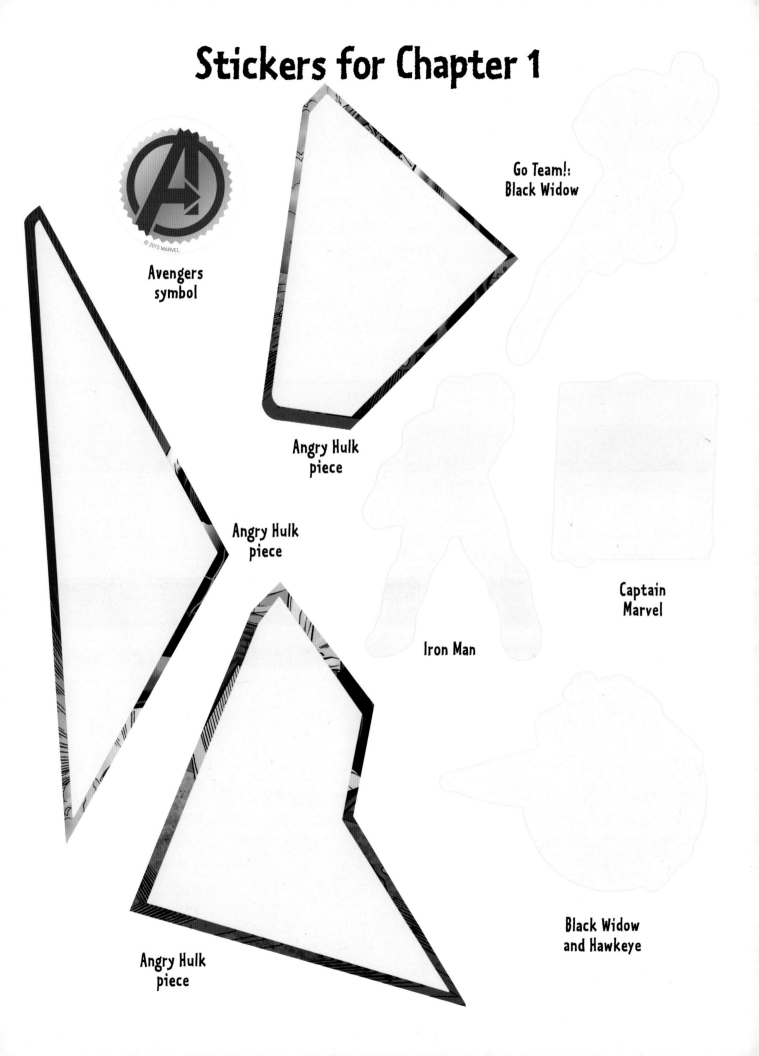

Stickers for Chapter 1

Avengers
symbol

Go Team!:
Black Widow

Angry Hulk
piece

Angry Hulk
piece

Angry Hulk
piece

Iron Man

Captain
Marvel

Black Widow
and Hawkeye

Stickers for Chapter 1

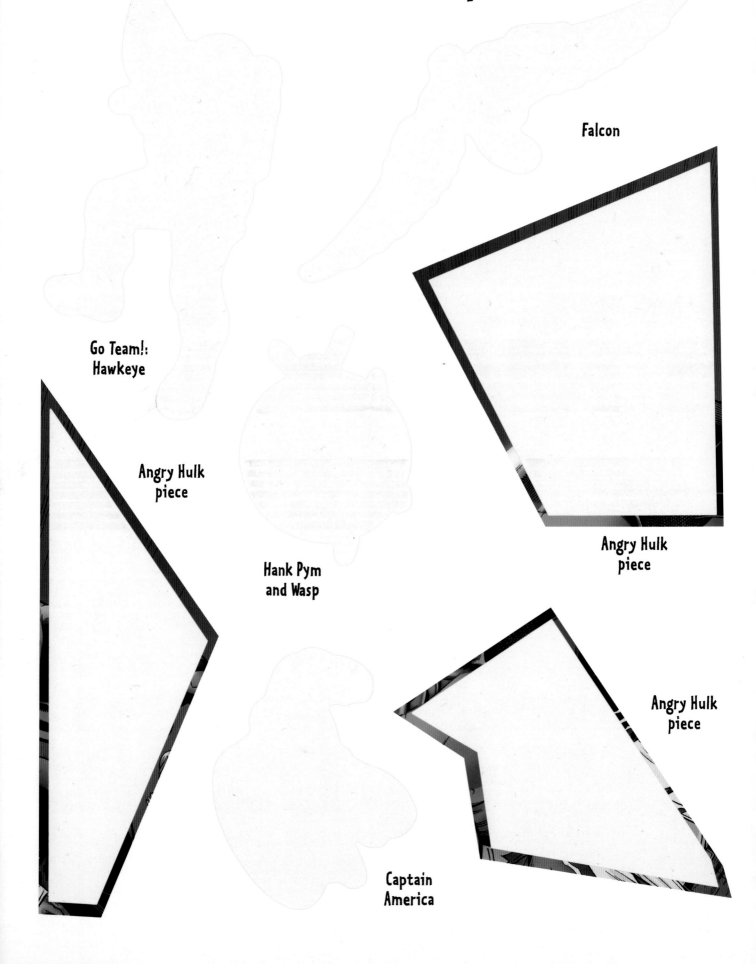

Falcon

Go Team!:
Hawkeye

Angry Hulk
piece

Hank Pym
and Wasp

Angry Hulk
piece

Angry Hulk
piece

Captain
America

Extra stickers

Thor

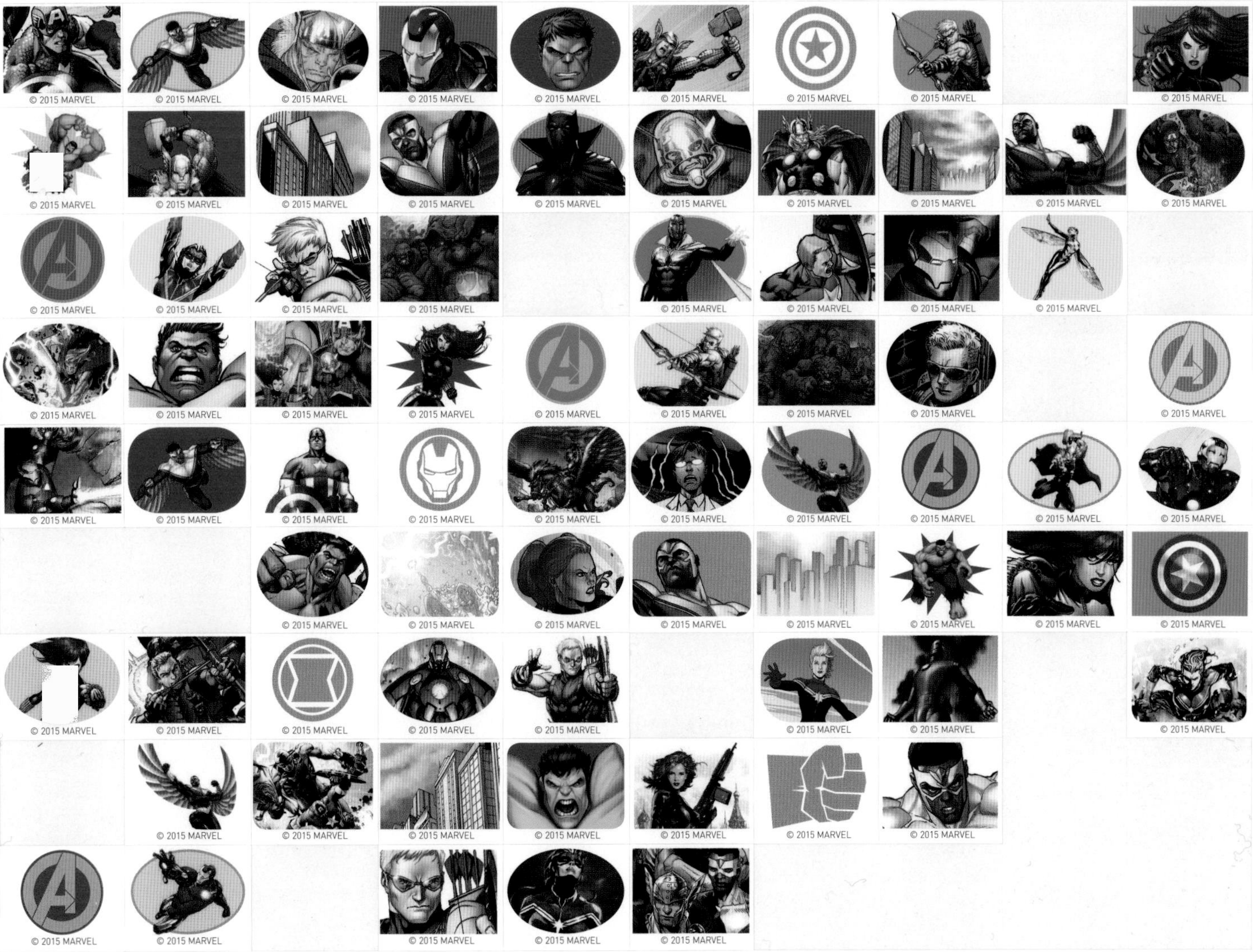
© 2015 MARVEL

Stickers for Chapter 2

Captain Marvel

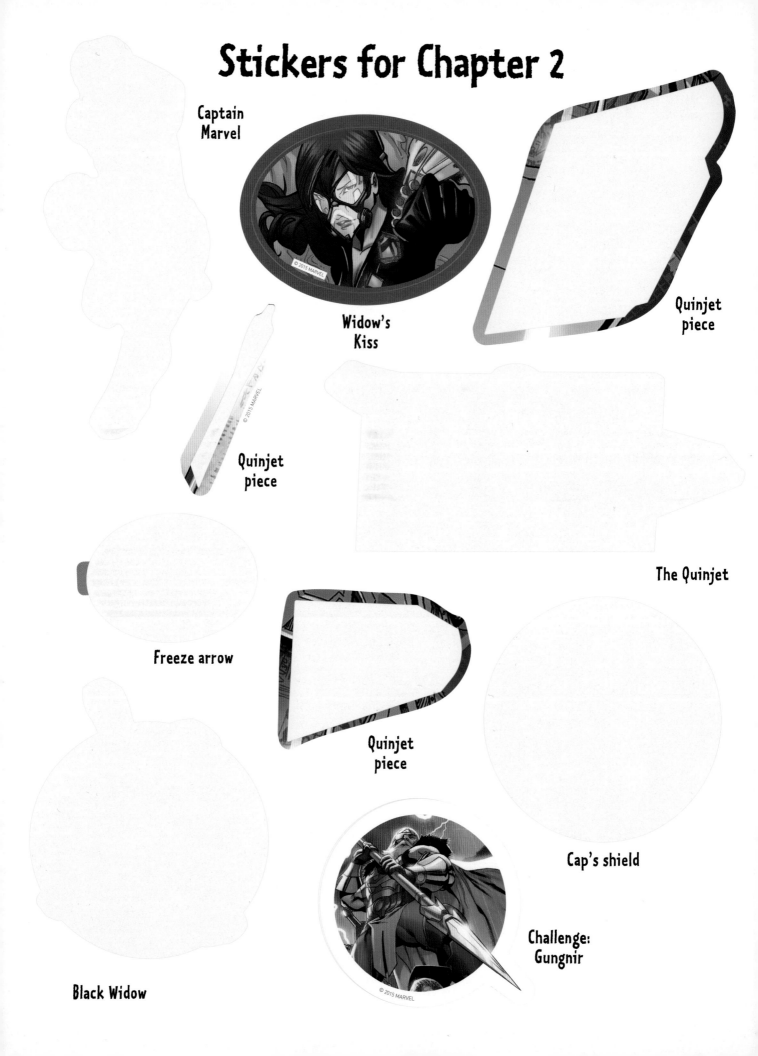

Widow's Kiss

Quinjet piece

Quinjet piece

The Quinjet

Freeze arrow

Quinjet piece

Cap's shield

Challenge: Gungnir

Black Widow

Stickers for Chapter 2

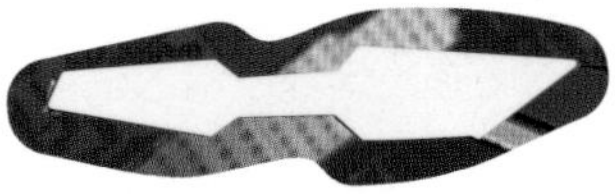

Quinjet piece

Hawkeye

Thor's hammer

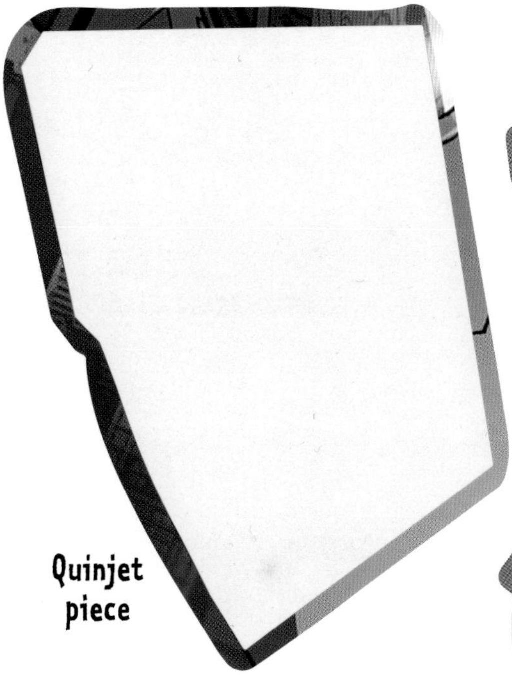

Cluster arrow

Avenger Profile: Captain Marvel

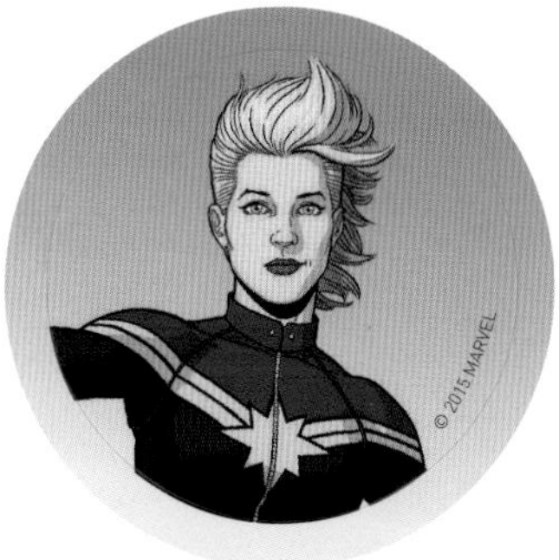
© 2015 MARVEL

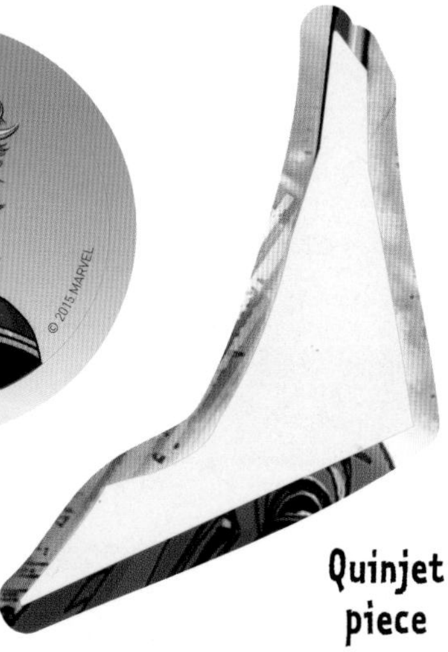

Quinjet piece

Portal arrow

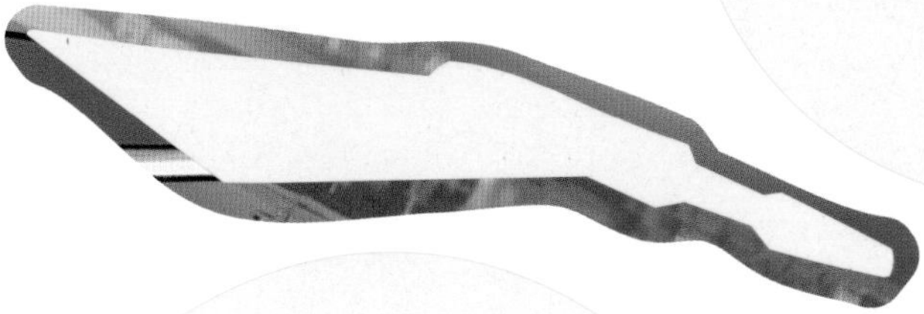

Quinjet piece

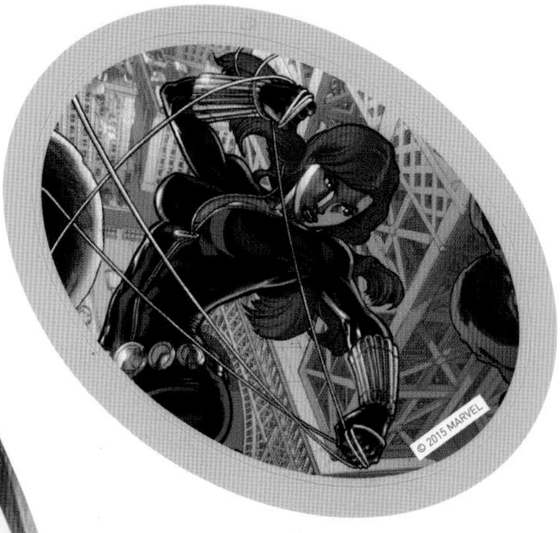
© 2015 MARVEL

Widow's Line

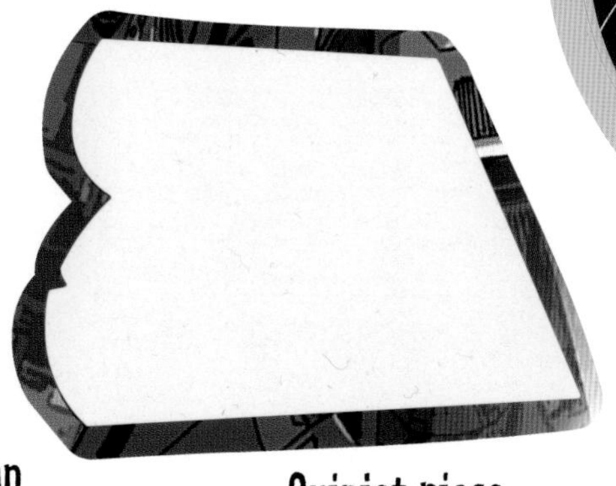

Asgardian technology

Quinjet piece

Stickers for Chapter 2

Quinjet
piece

Widow's
Bite

Hulk punch
arrow

Quinjet
piece

Quinjet
piece

Quinjet
piece

Extra stickers

Extra stickers

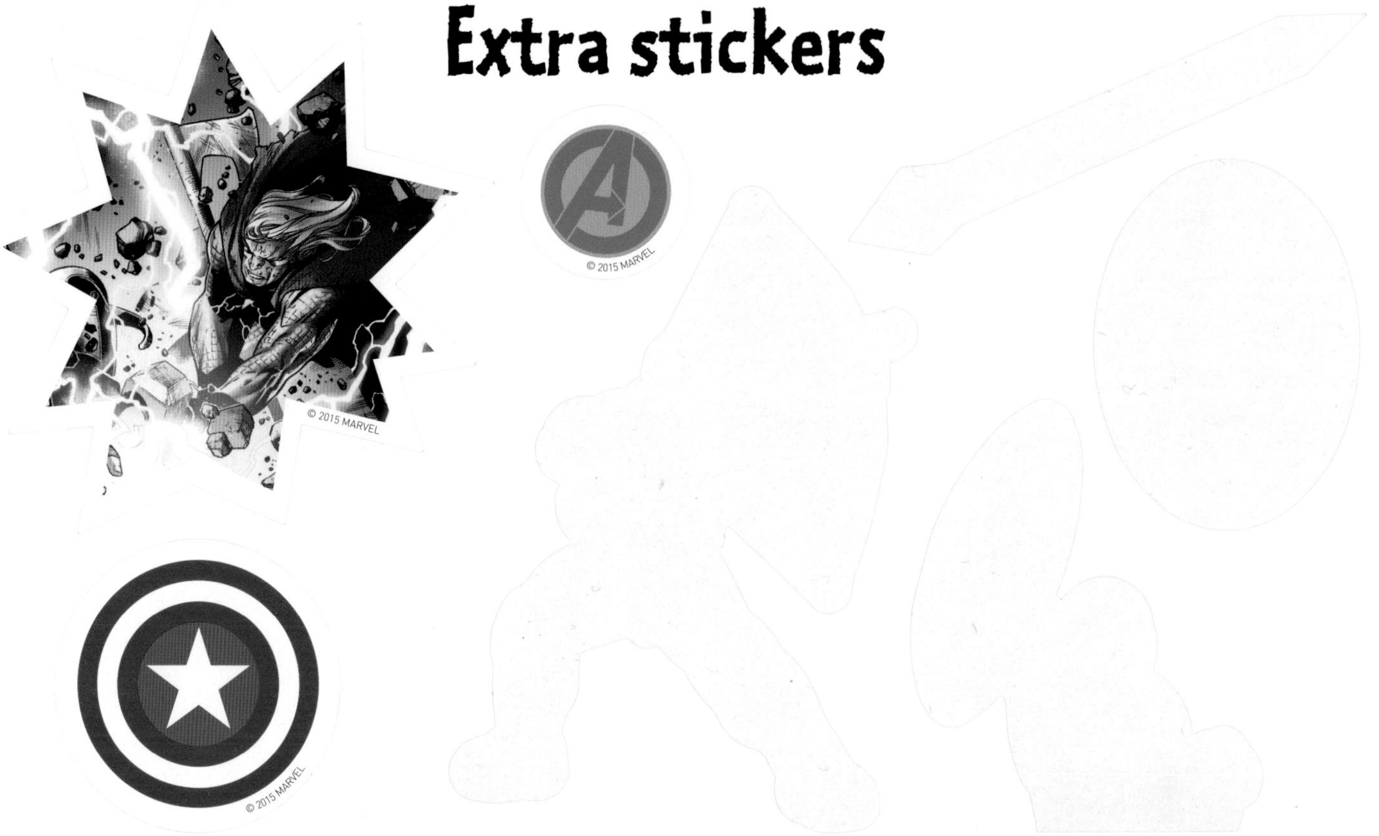
© 2015 MARVEL

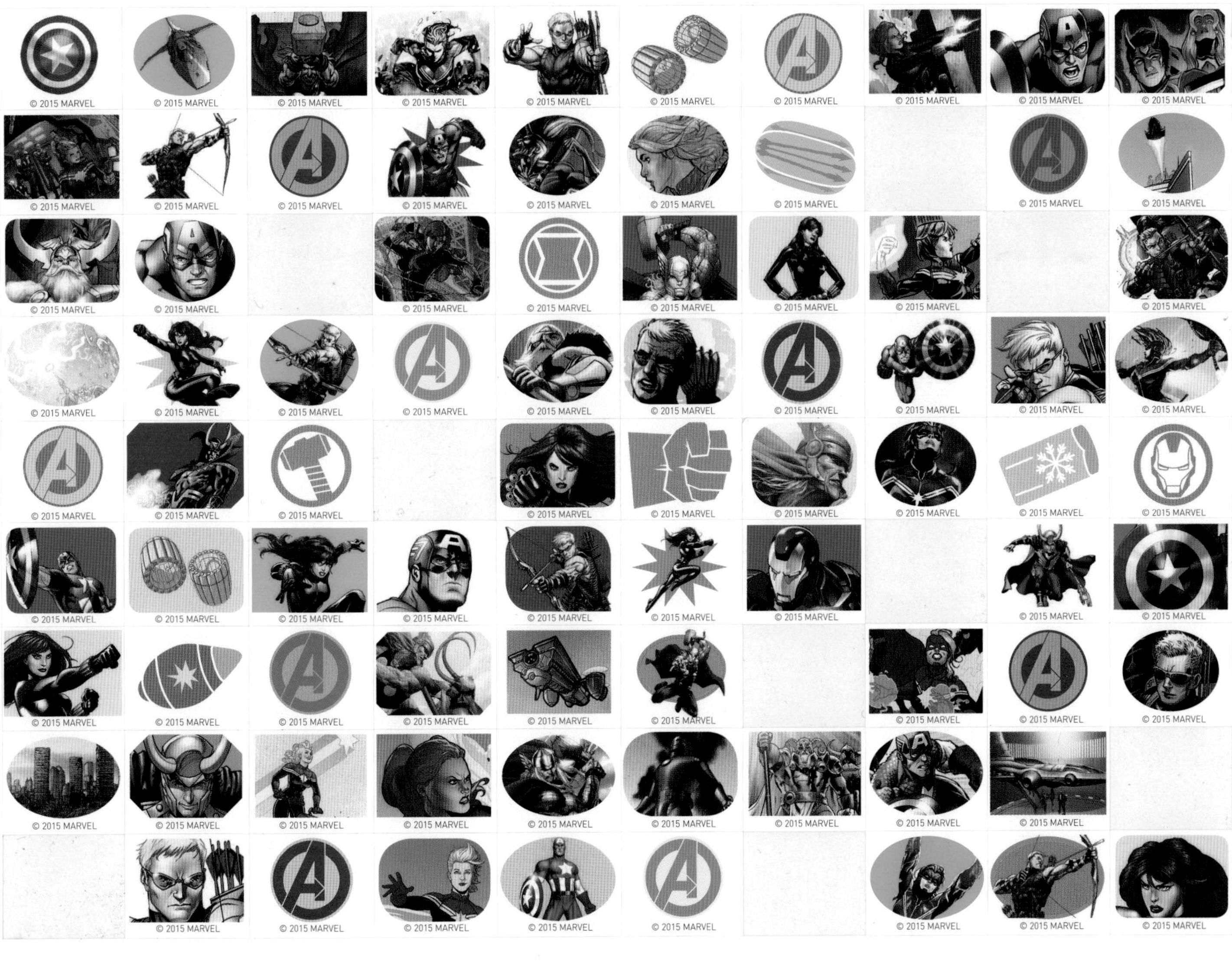
© 2015 MARVEL

Stickers for Chapter 3

Evil Villains:
Attuma

Baron Zemo

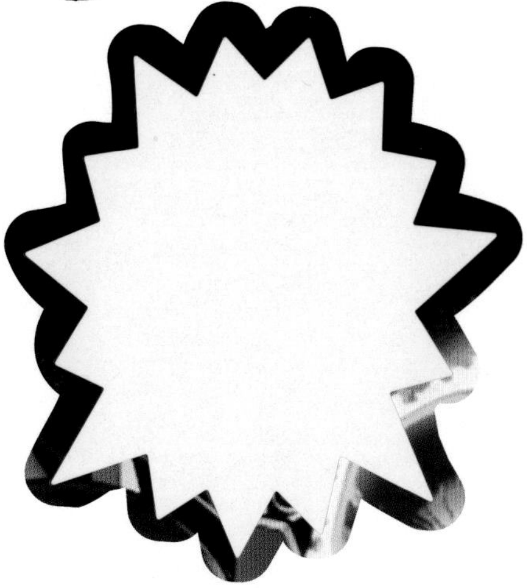

Black Knight!

Thanos

Evil Villains:
Egghead

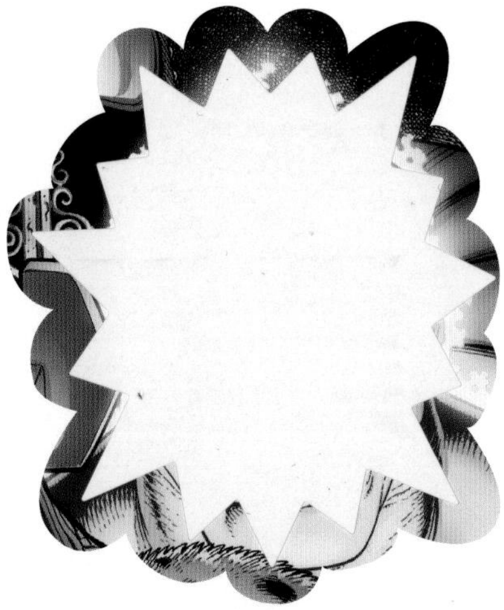

Radioactive
Man!

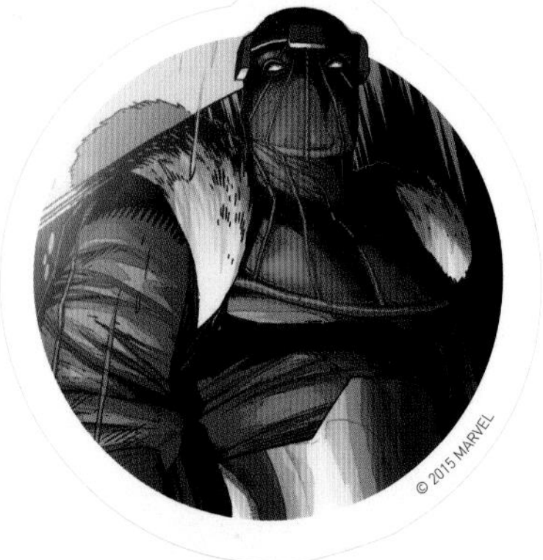
© 2015 MARVEL

Challenge:
Baron Zemo

Evil Villains:
Ultron

The Masters of Evil

Stickers for Chapter 3

Attuma

Evil Villains:
Baron Zemo

Loki

Melter!

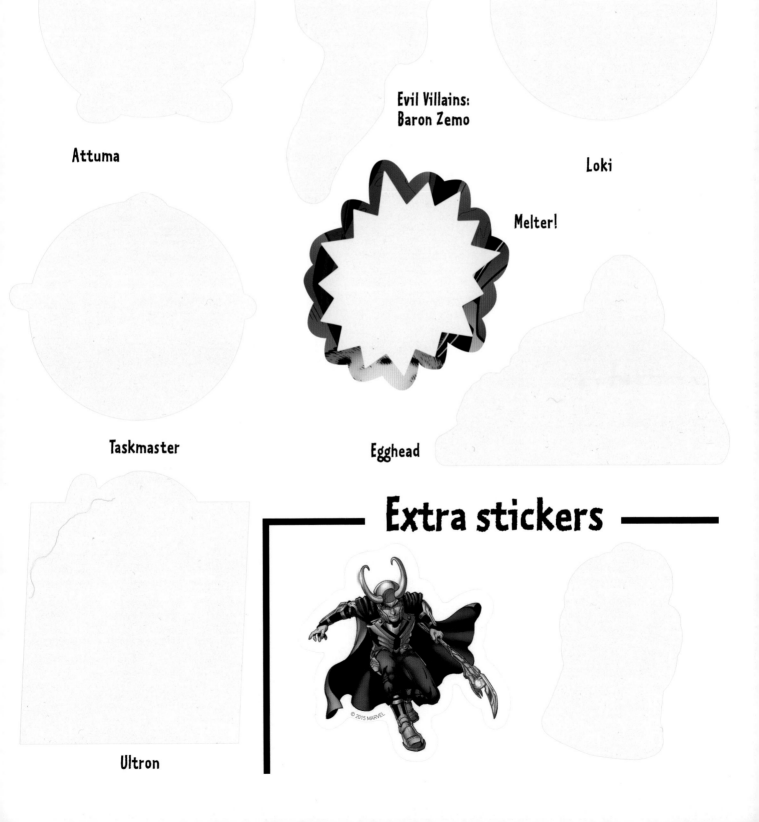

Taskmaster

Egghead

Extra stickers

Ultron

© 2015 MARVEL

Extra stickers

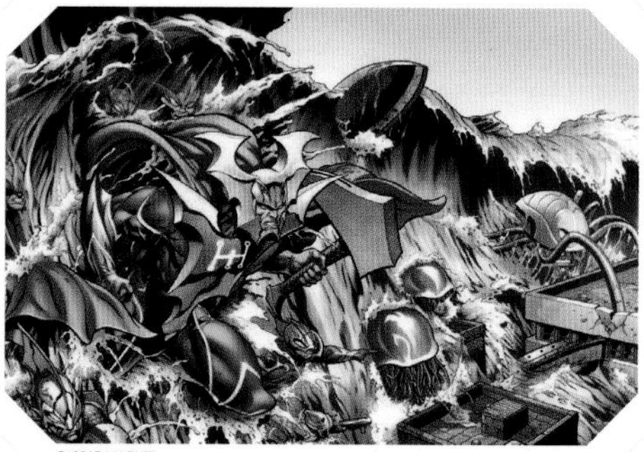

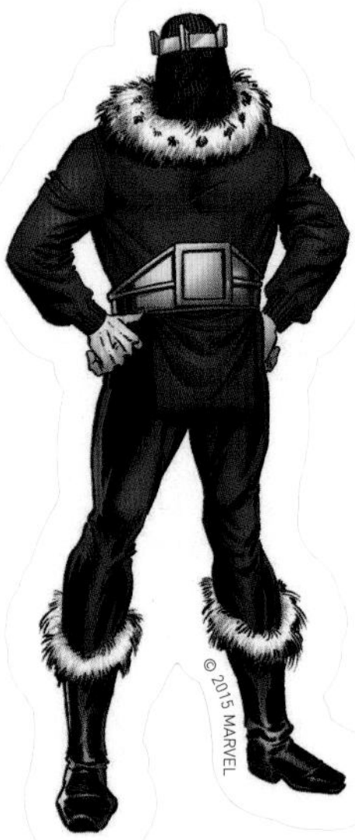

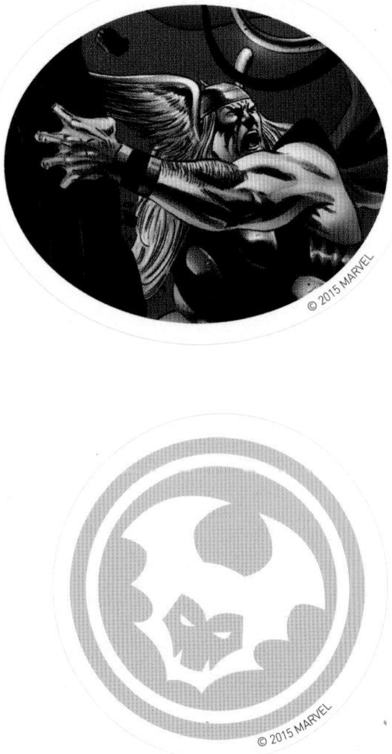

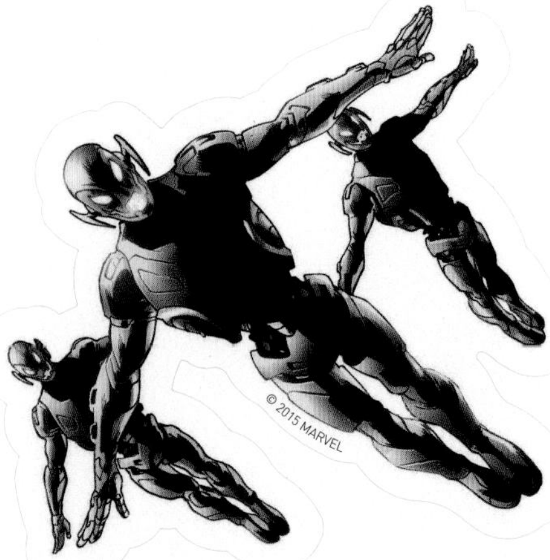

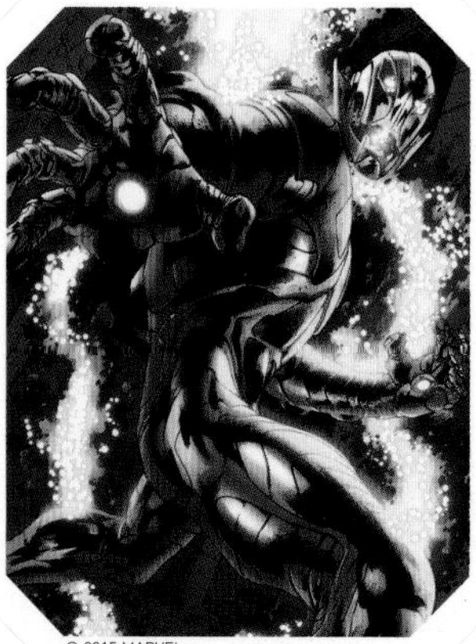

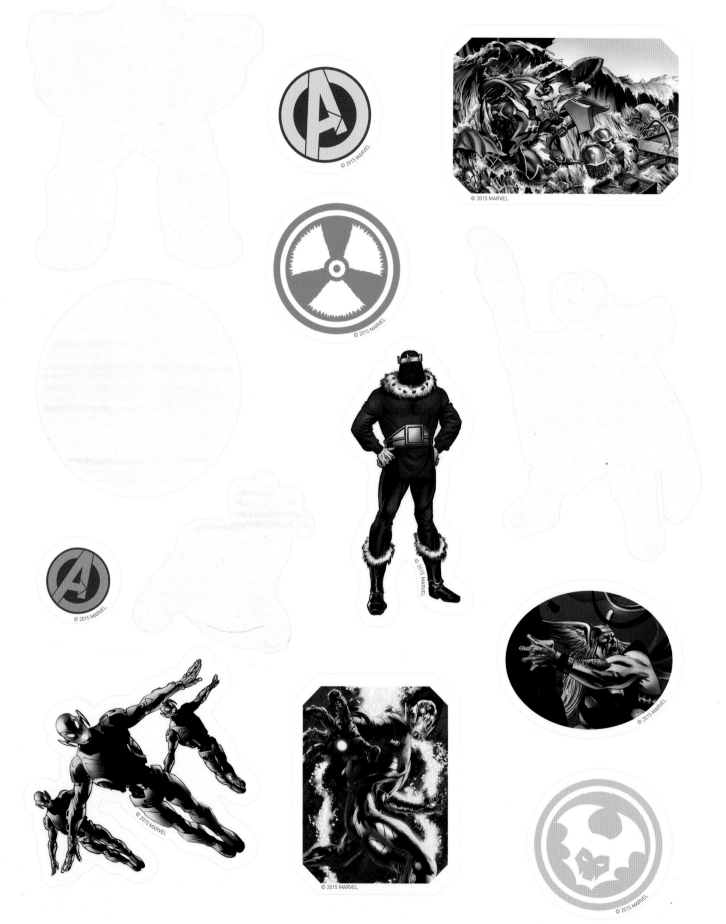

Extra stickers

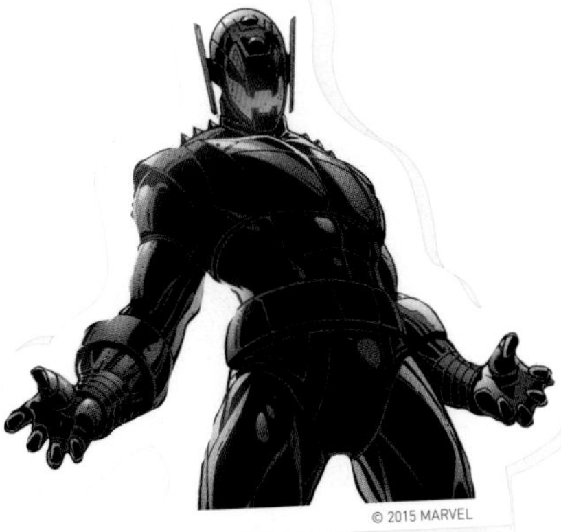
© 2015 MARVEL

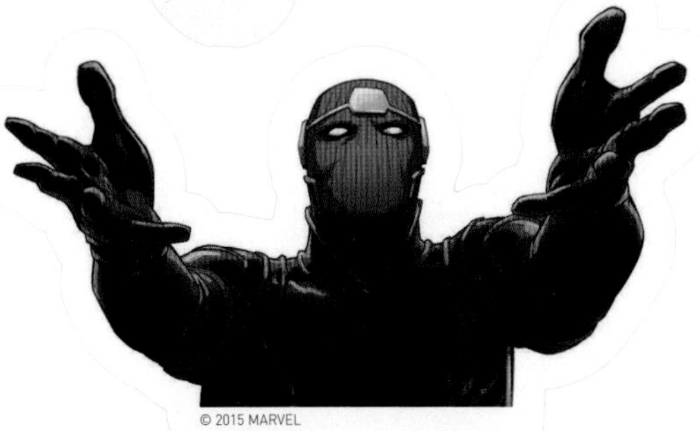
© 2015 MARVEL

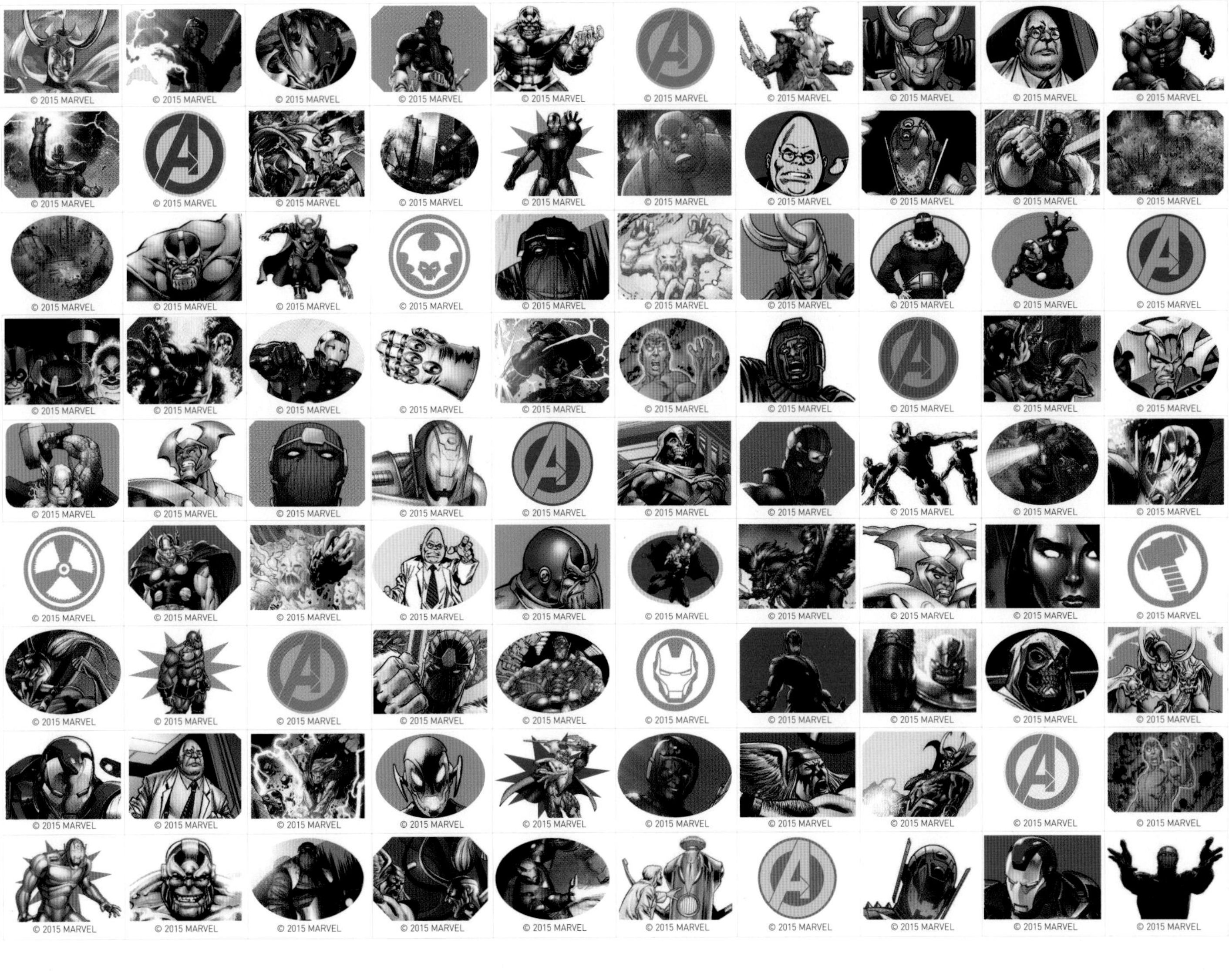
© 2015 MARVEL

Stickers for Chapter 4

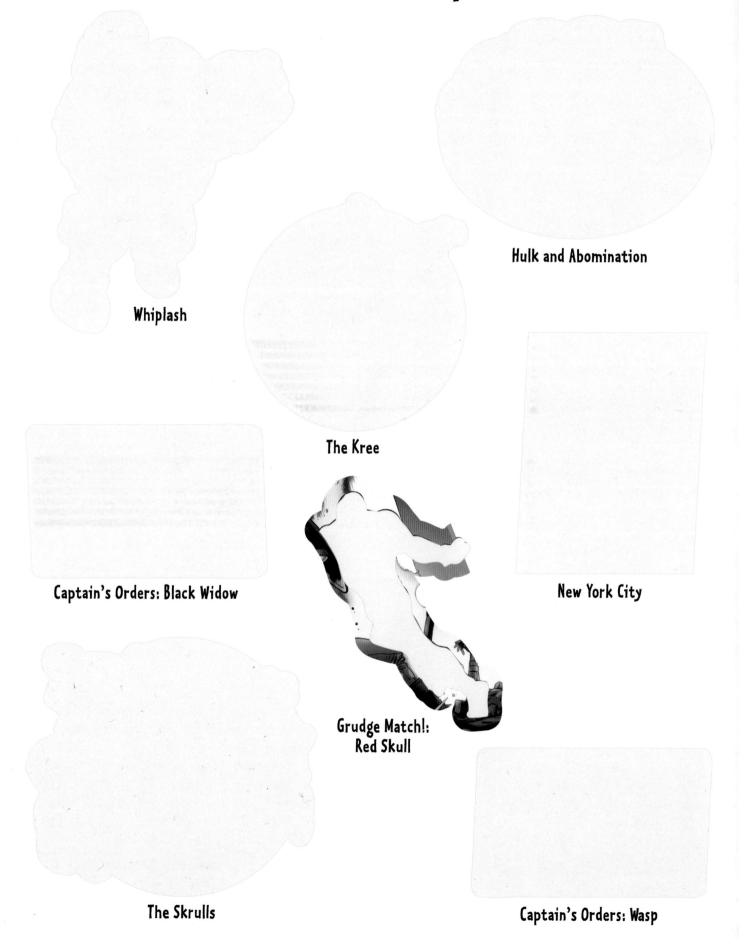

Whiplash

Hulk and Abomination

The Kree

Captain's Orders: Black Widow

New York City

Grudge Match!:
Red Skull

The Skrulls

Captain's Orders: Wasp

Stickers for Chapter 4

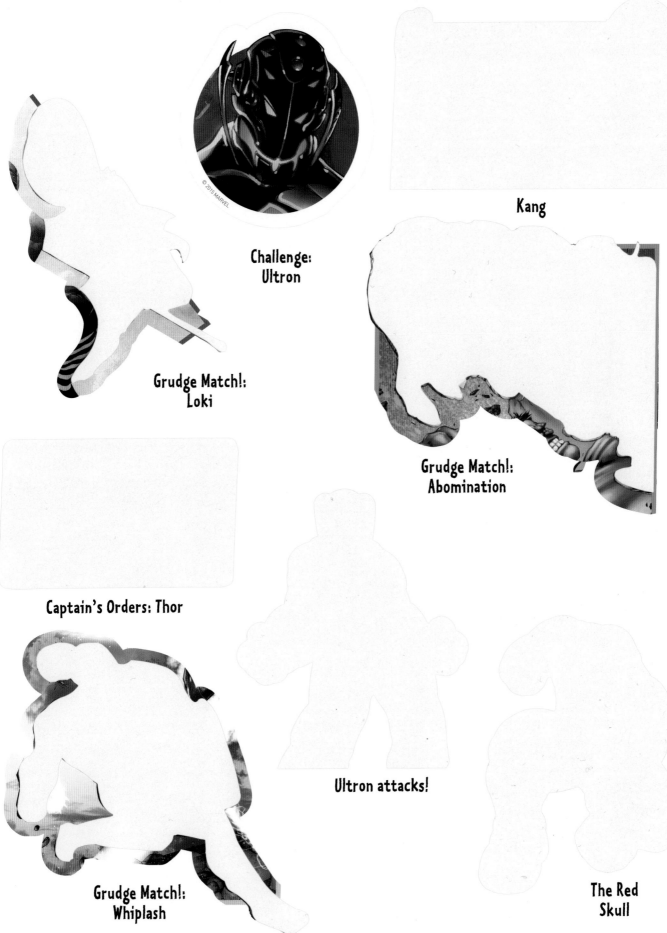

Kang

Challenge: Ultron

Grudge Match!: Loki

Grudge Match!: Abomination

Captain's Orders: Thor

Grudge Match!: Whiplash

Ultron attacks!

The Red Skull

Extra stickers

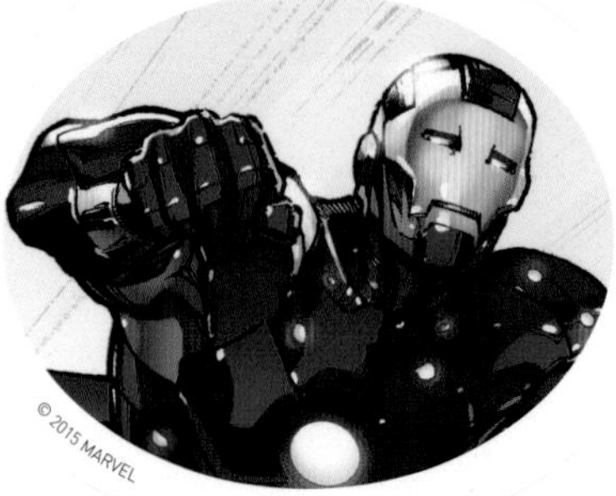
© 2015 MARVEL

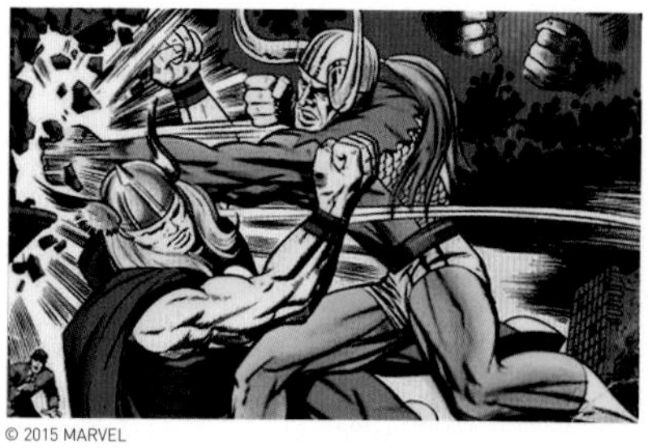
© 2015 MARVEL

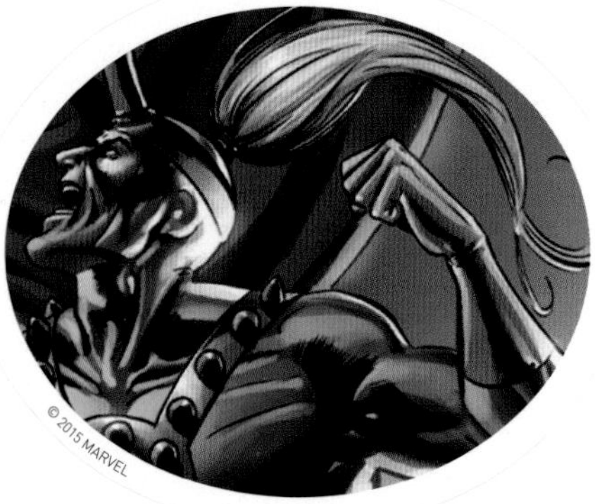
© 2015 MARVEL

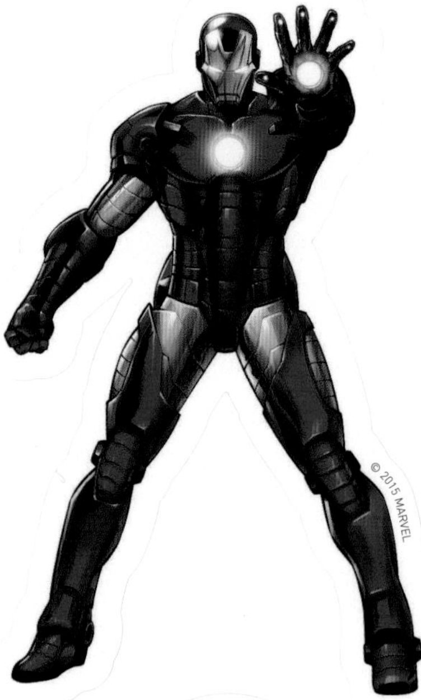
© 2015 MARVEL

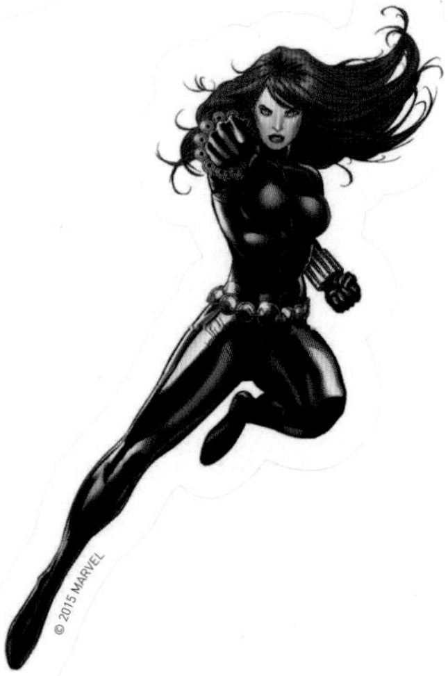
© 2015 MARVEL

Extra stickers

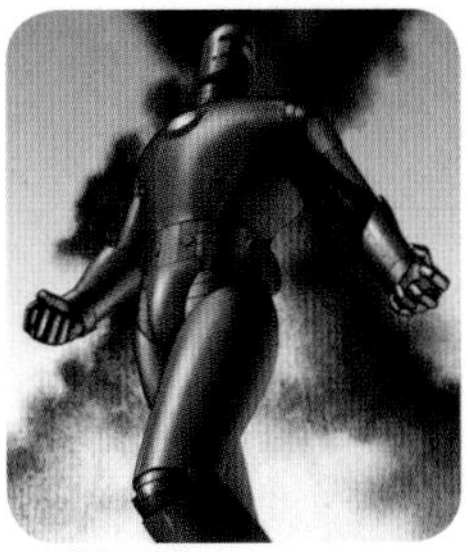

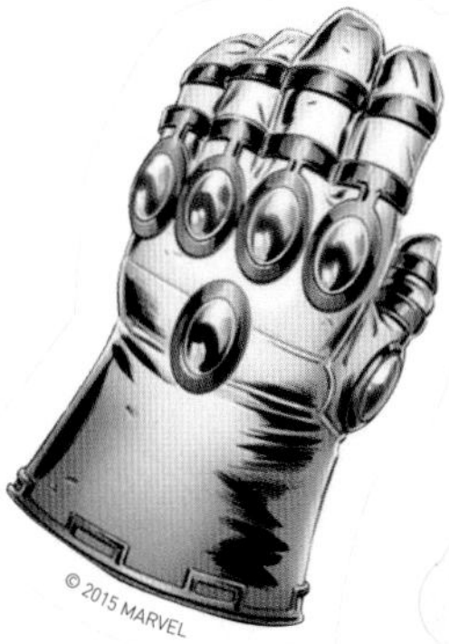

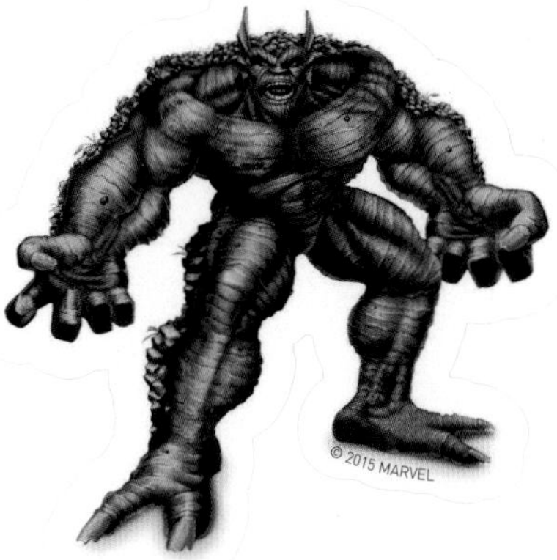

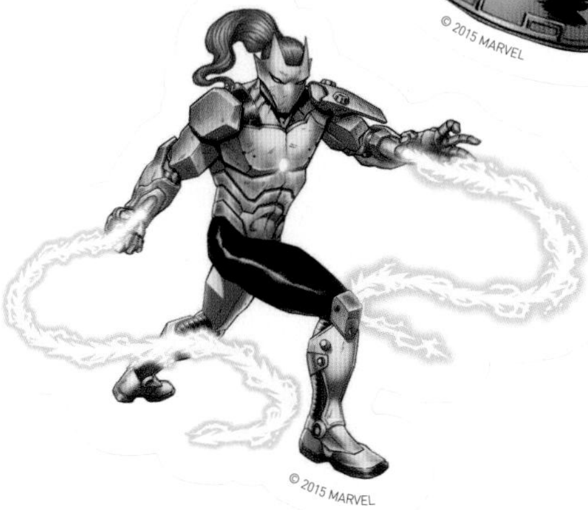

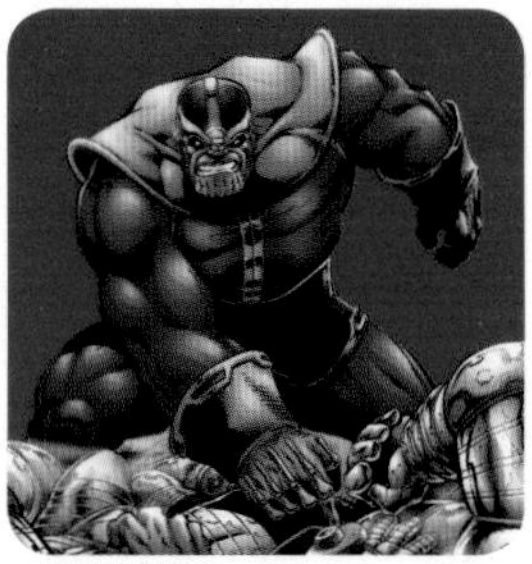

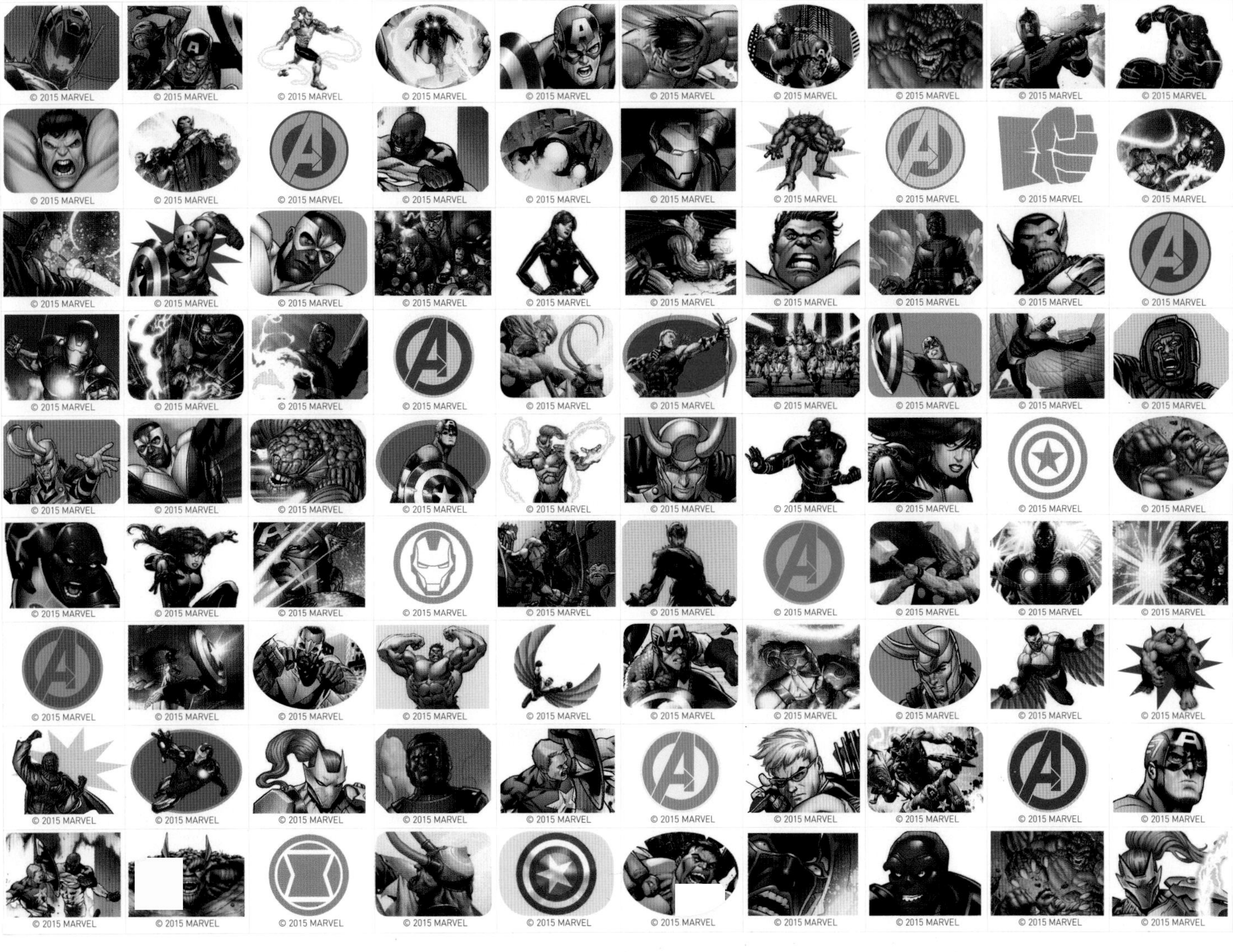

© 2015 MARVEL